Published by
"GDG"
Global Doodle Gems

IMAGI WORLD

Book 1
by
Maria Wedel

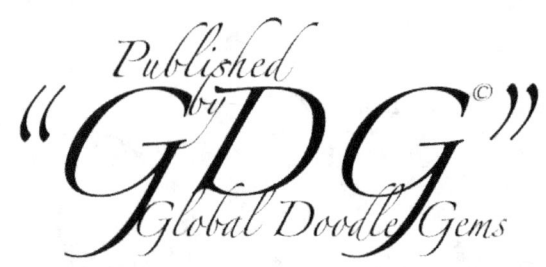

Share your colored versions with us ! We love seeing your results and hearing from you we are social !

The Official FB book page, stay on top of what we have in the works !
www.facebook.com/globaldoodlegems
The Community group, share your colored pages, meet the artists, enjoy exclusive freebies, take part in community Charity books and so much more......
www.facebook.com/groups/globaldoodlegems/
Follow us on Twitter.... @GlobalDoodlegem
We are on Instagram too
@globaldoodlegems for instagram
...and if you are not social like that we have a blog
globaldoodlegems.wordpress.com

Copyright © 2016 Global Doodle Gems
All rights are reserved by Global Doodle Gems.
Duplication of pages for personal use are allowed. You are invited to color the pages then scan/post your coloured versions to social networks, mentioning the book title and author/artist (Global Doodle Gems).
All artwork and images are protected by copyright laws. This book or any portion thereof may not, otherwise, be reproduced and/or distributed or transmitted without the express written permission of the artist/publisher of Global Doodle Gems.
All of us from the Global Doodle Gems wish you a colortastic time and look forward to seeing your wonderful color results online !

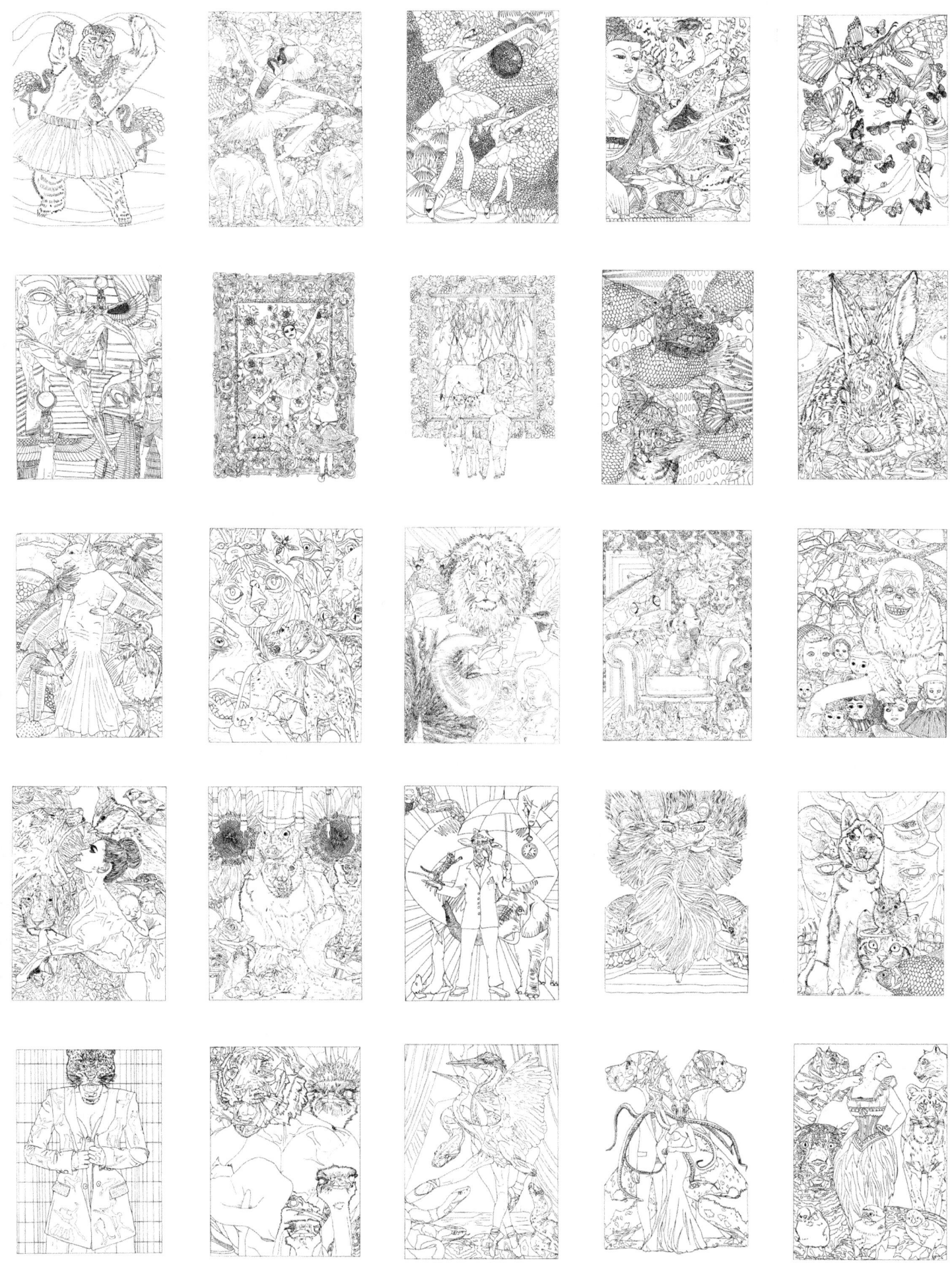

"BalletBear"

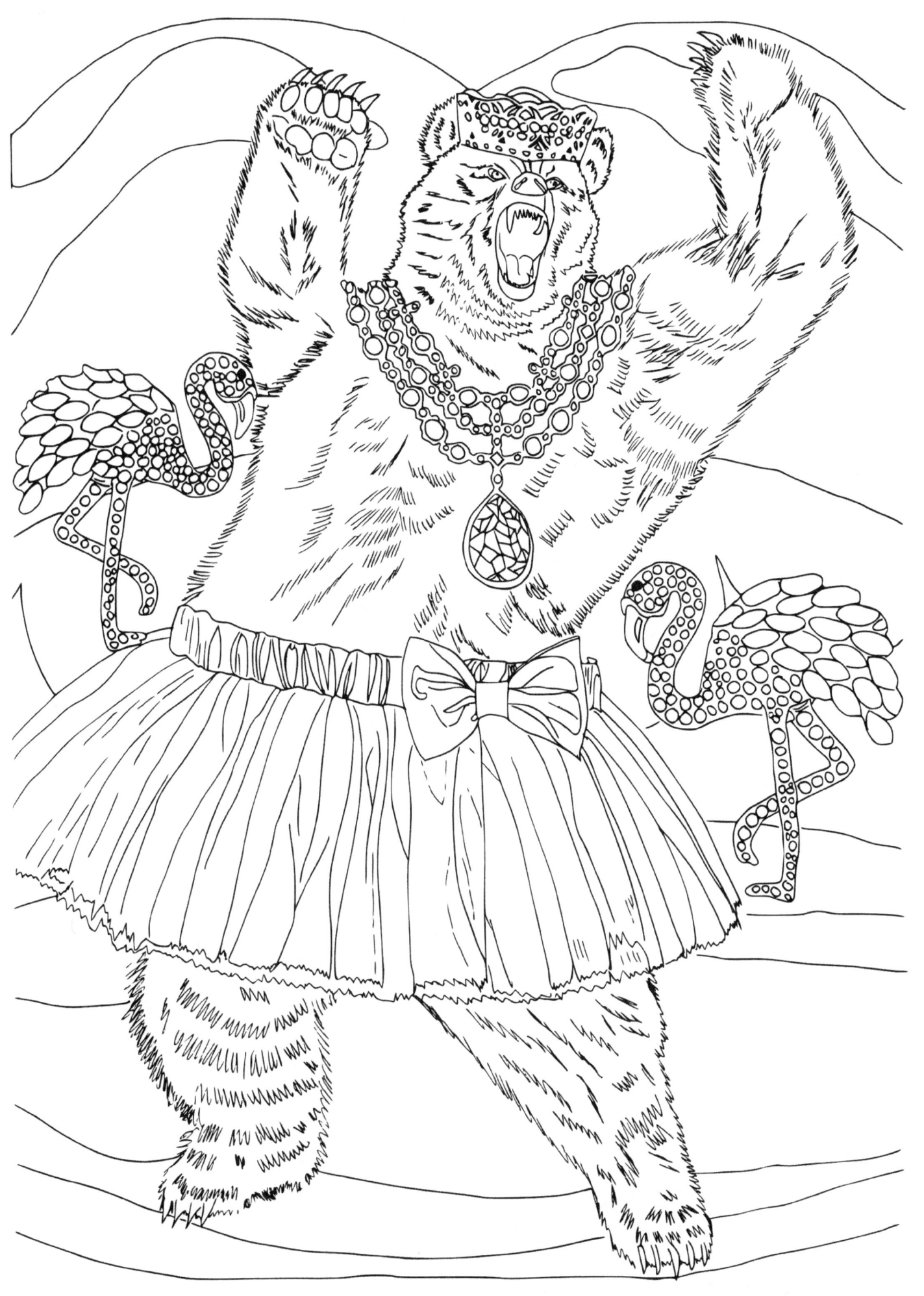

"BalletPhant"

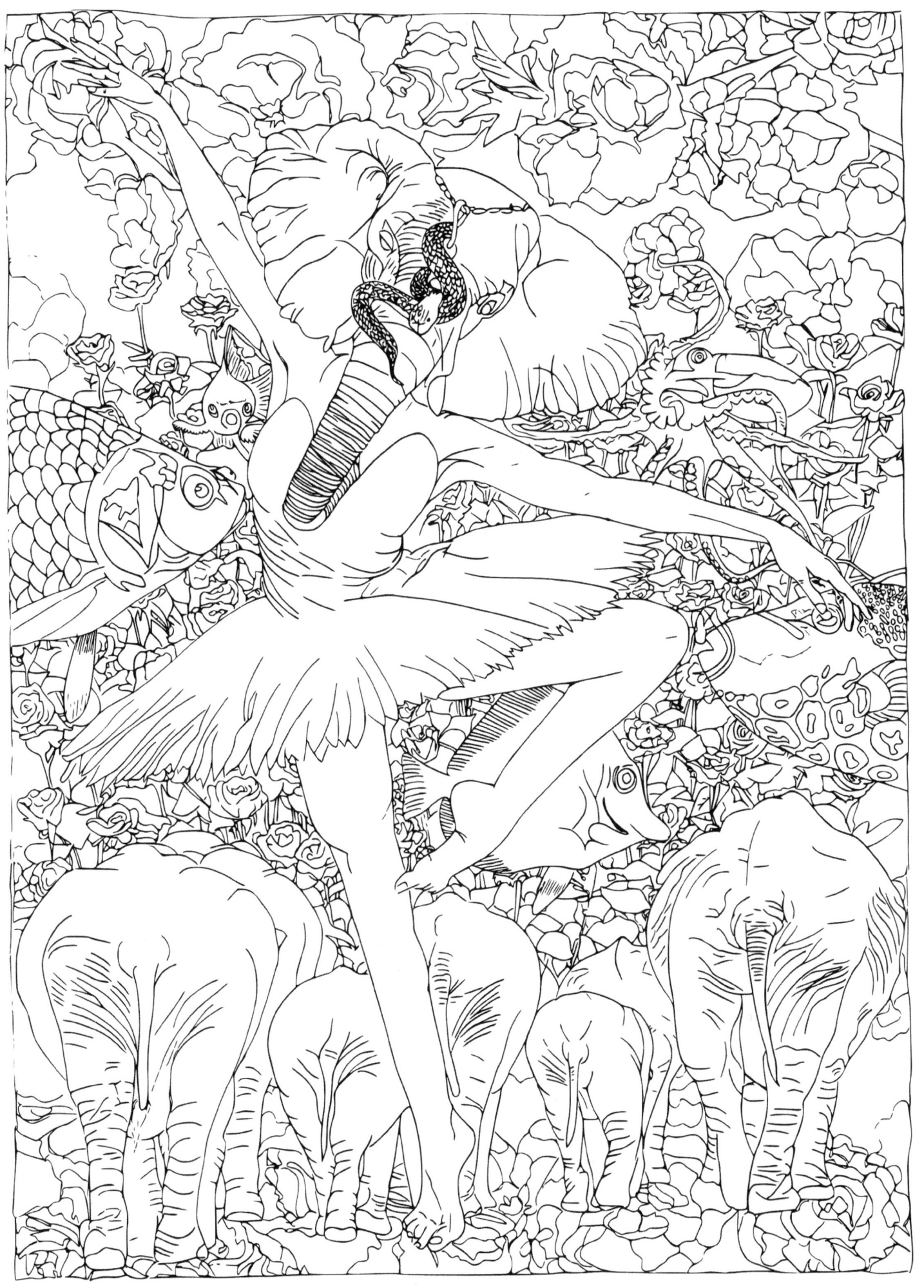

"BalletShark"

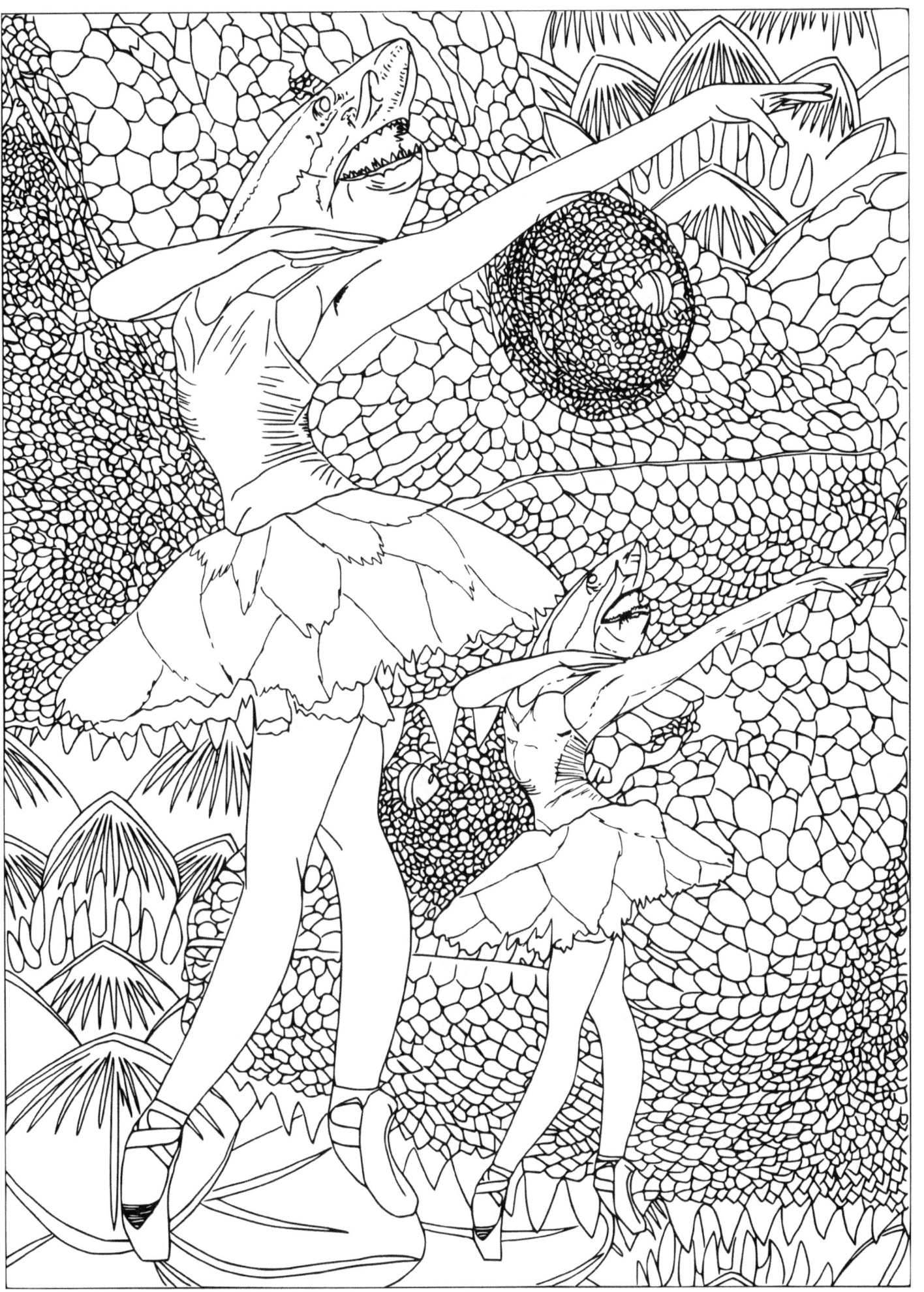

"BuddhaDreams"

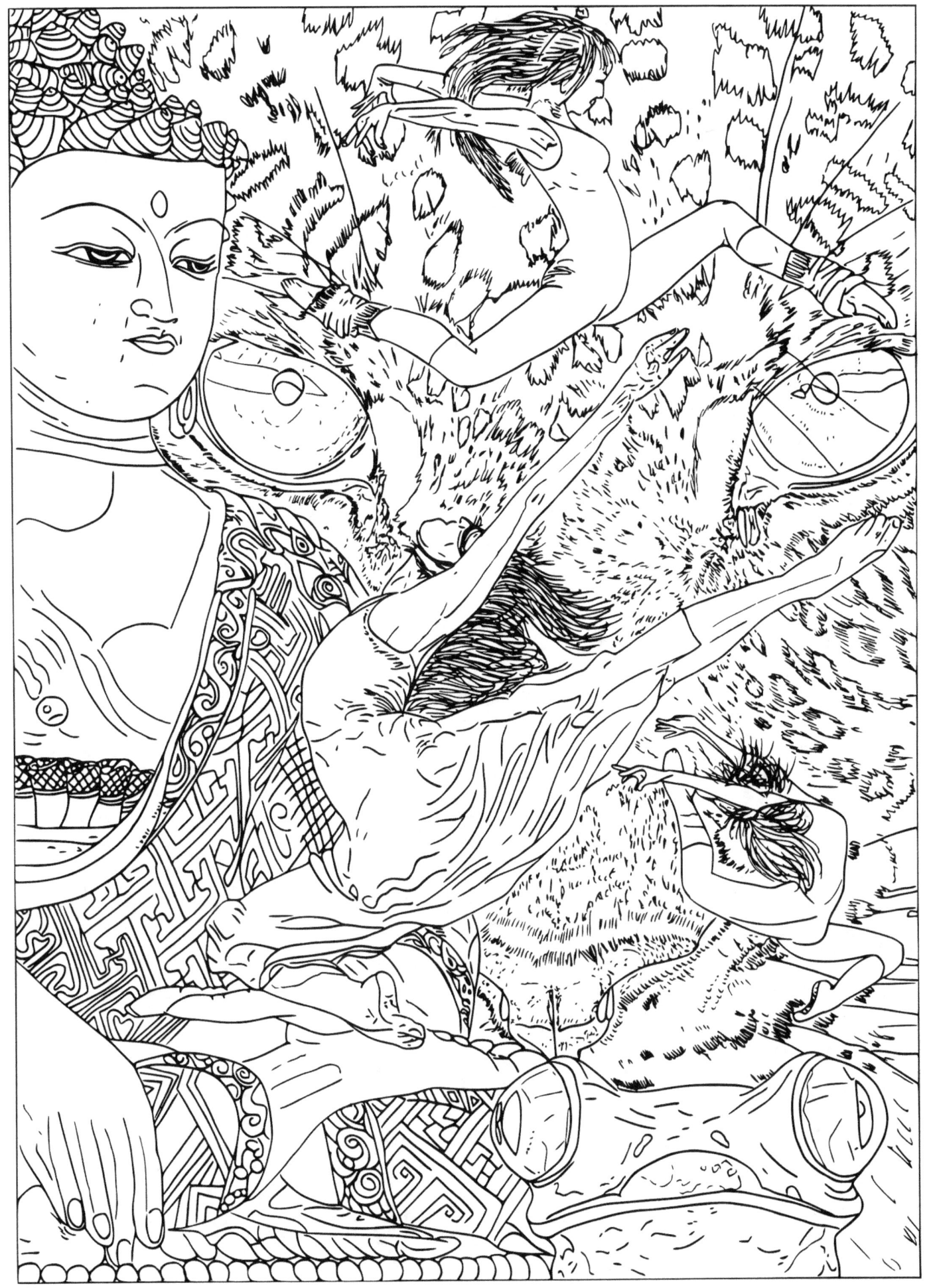

"Butterfly Attack"

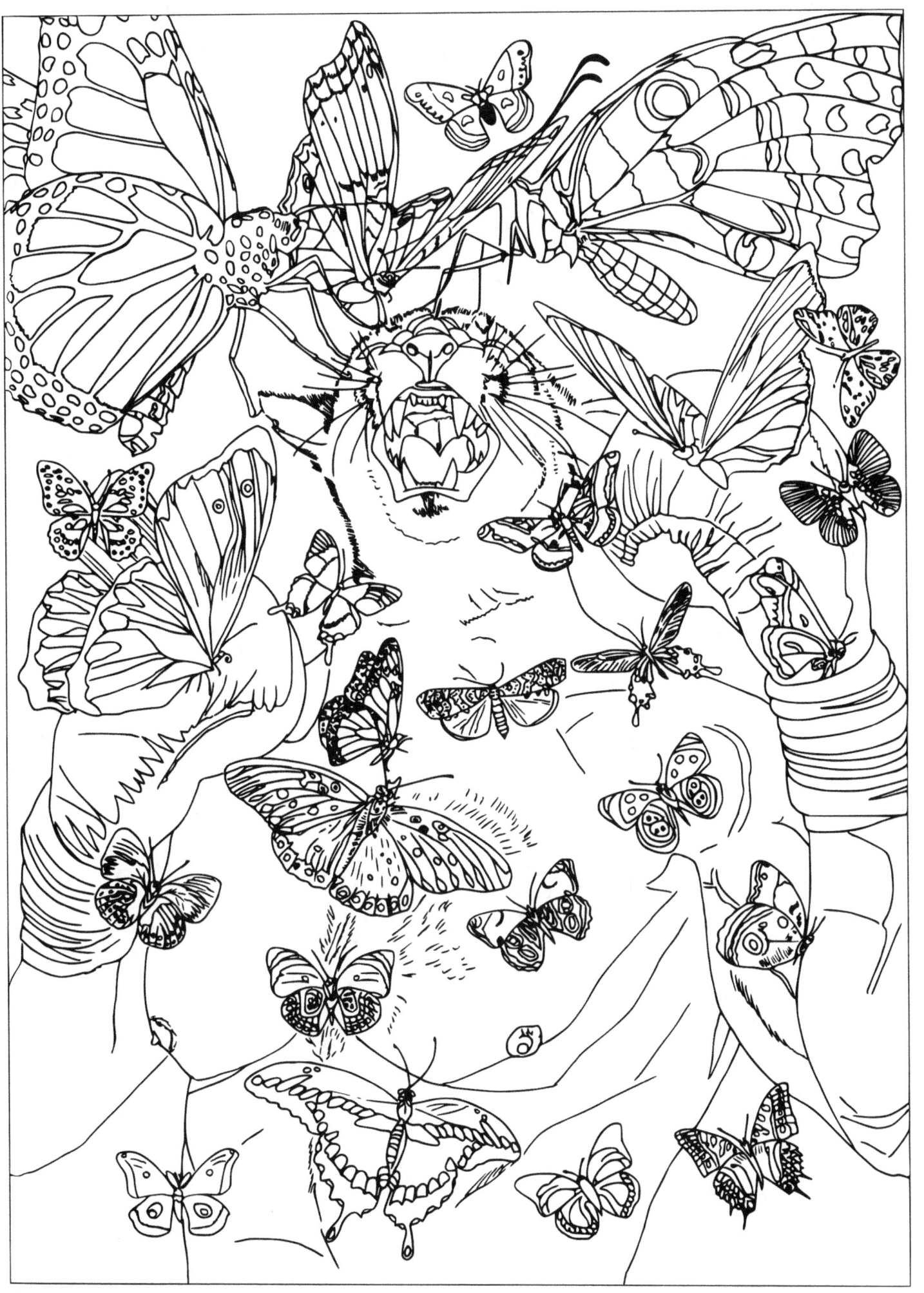

"Dancer"

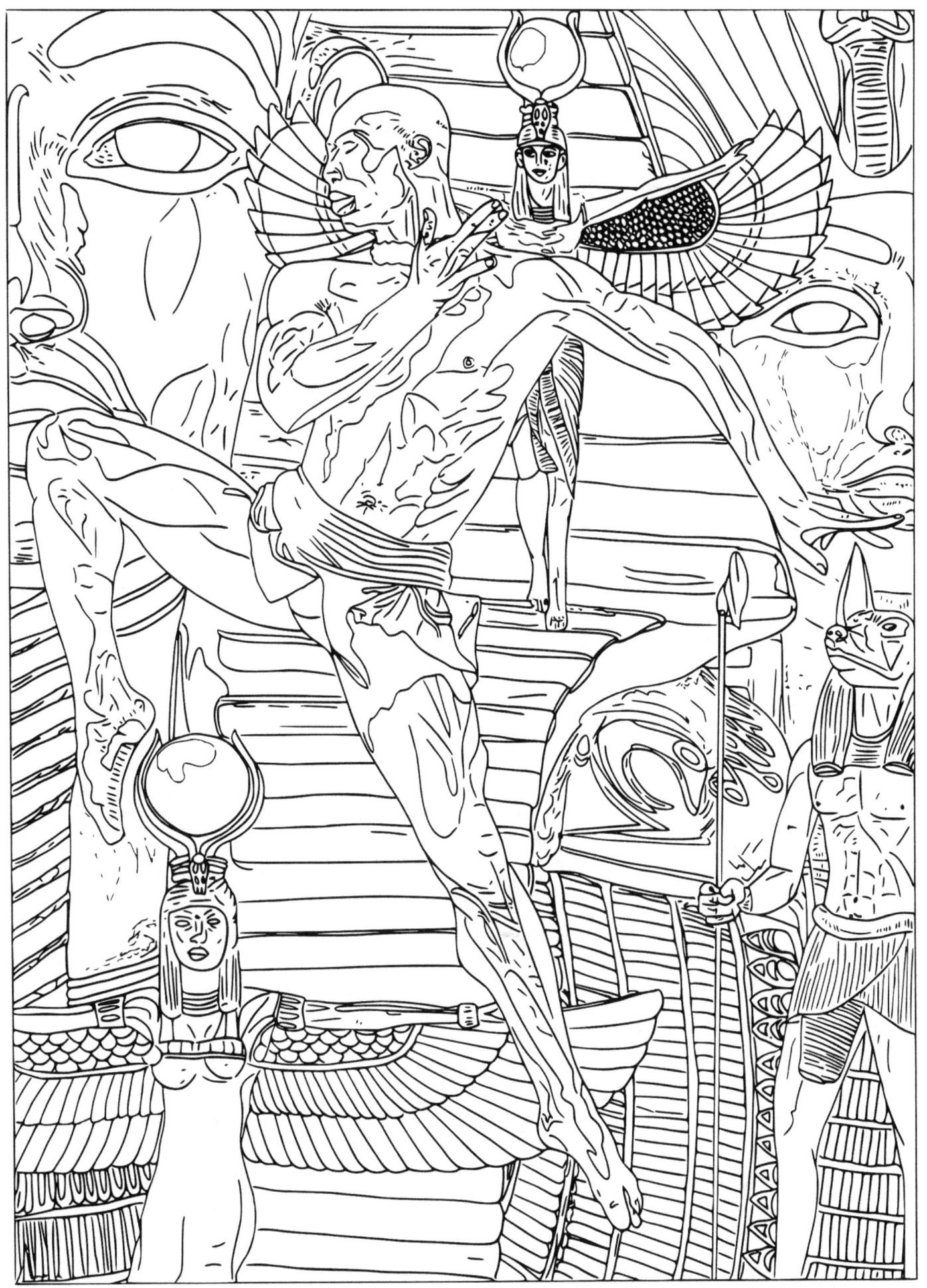

"DreamBig"

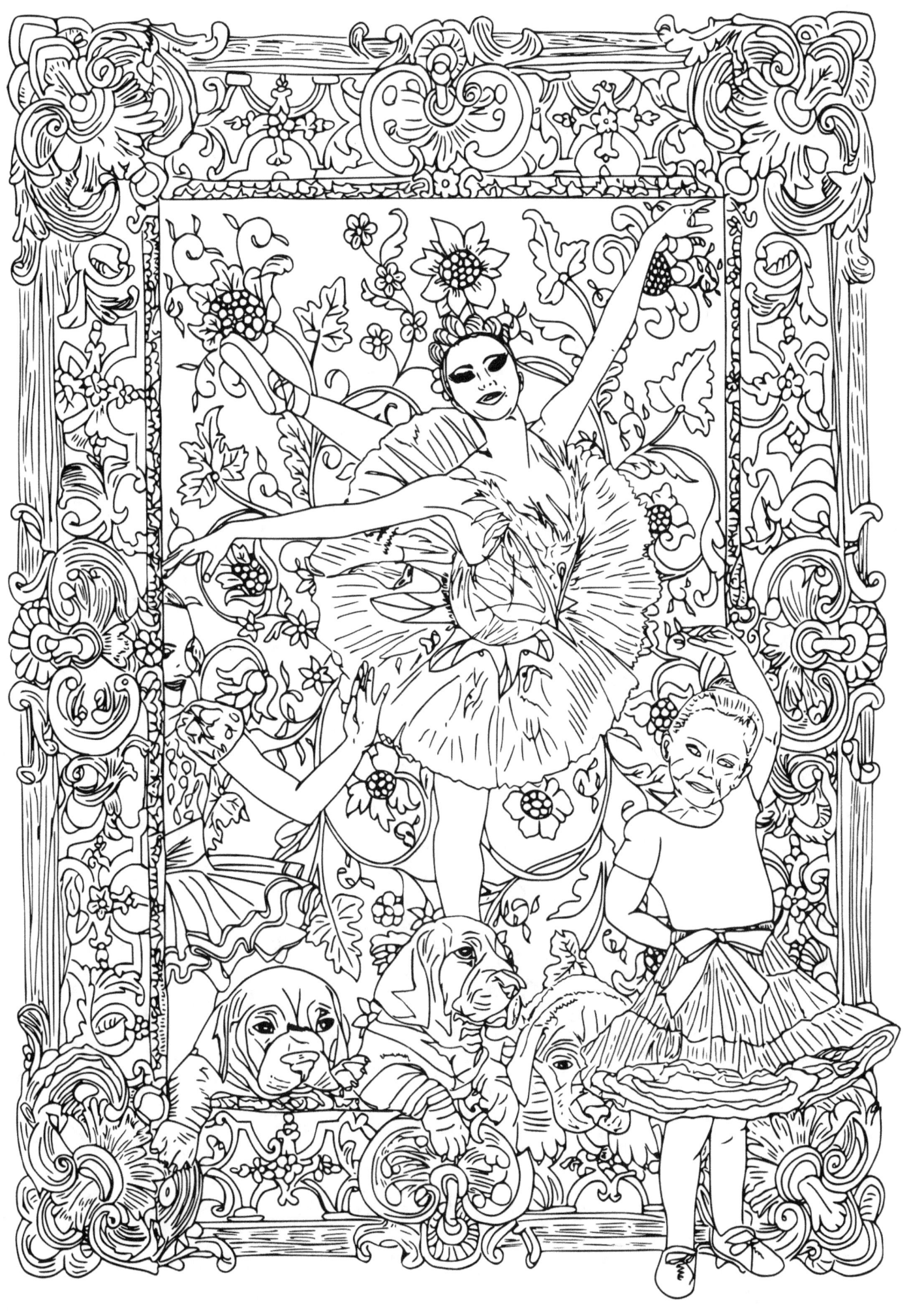

"Family"

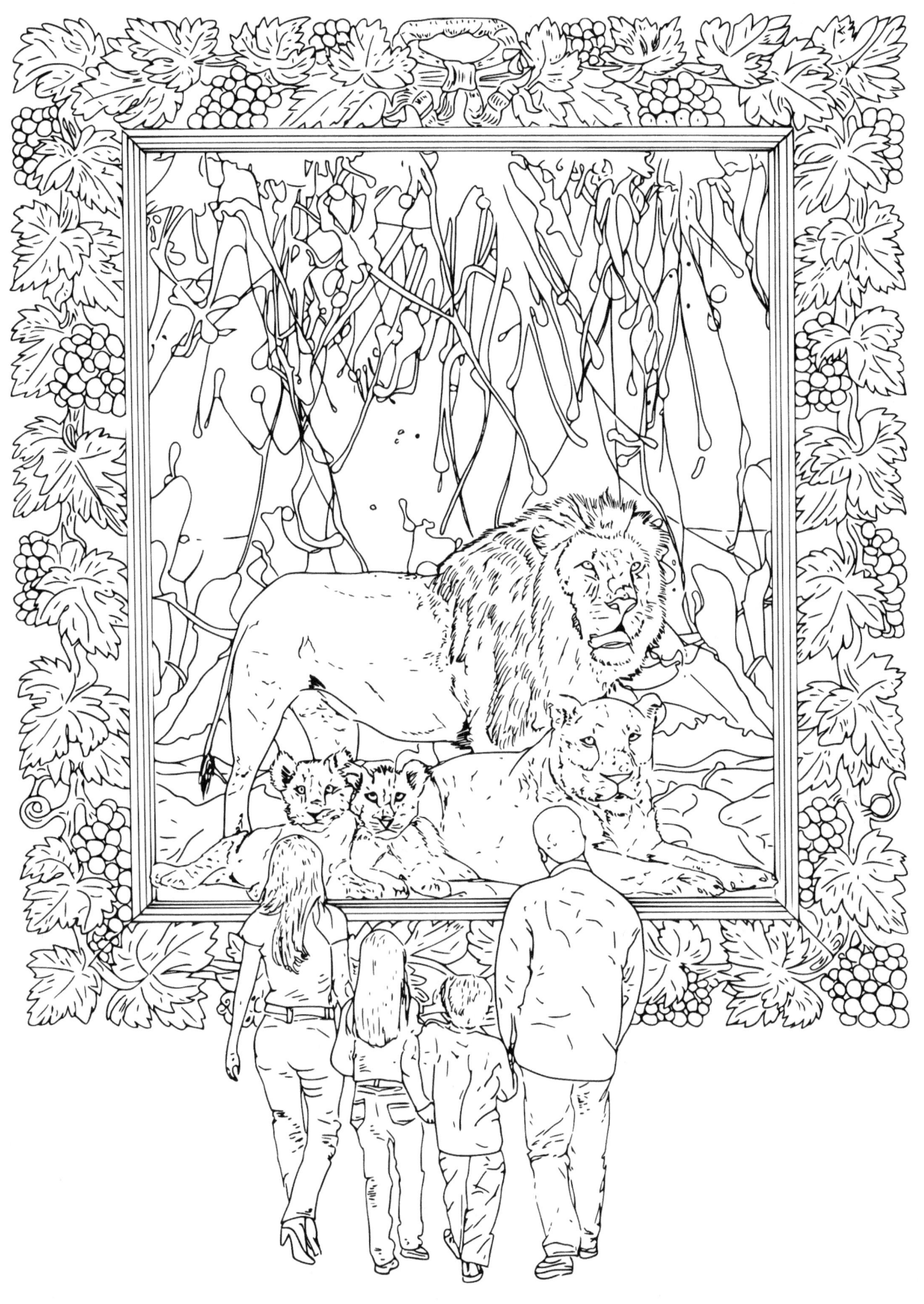

"Fishy Adventures"

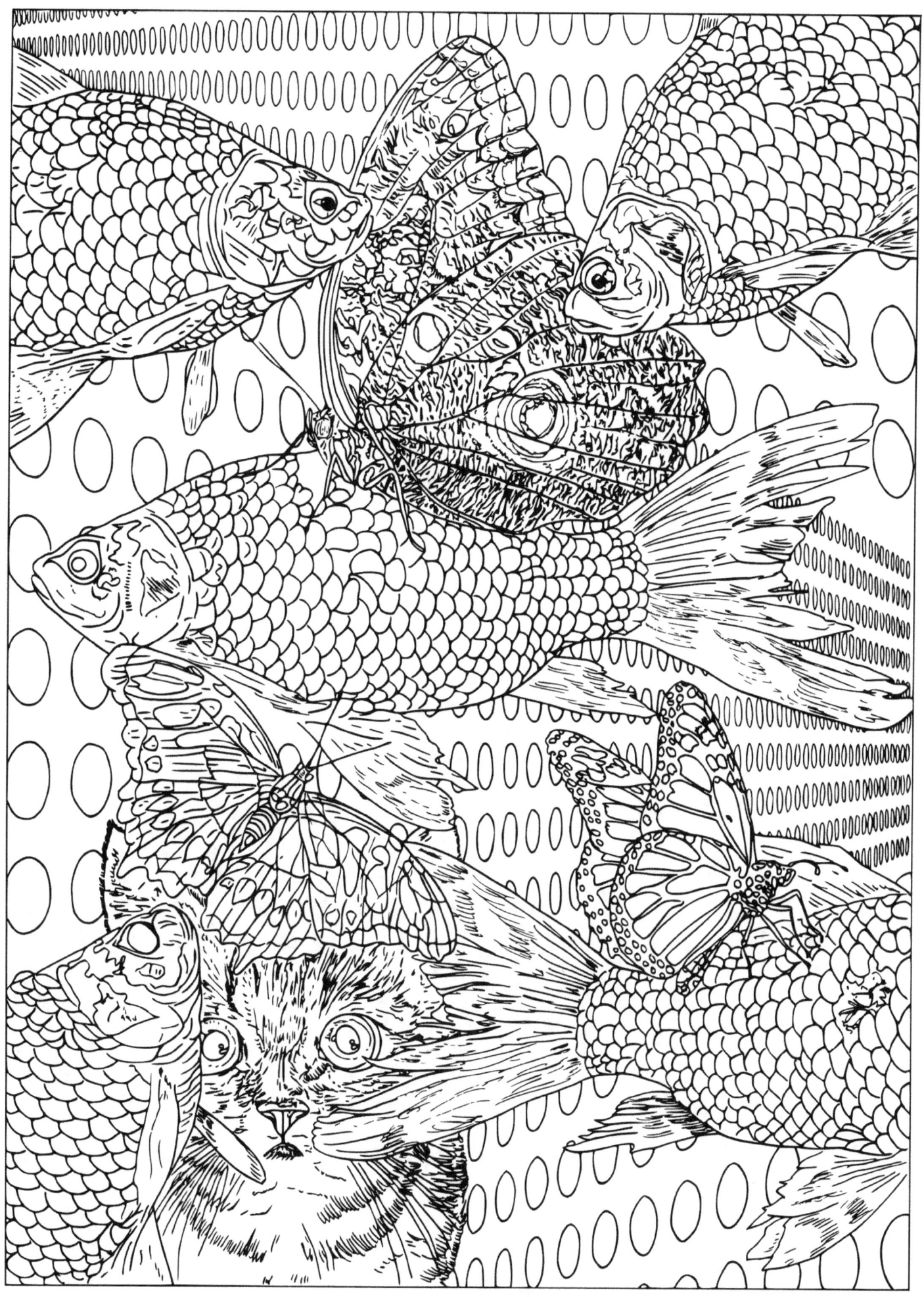

"Gigantico"

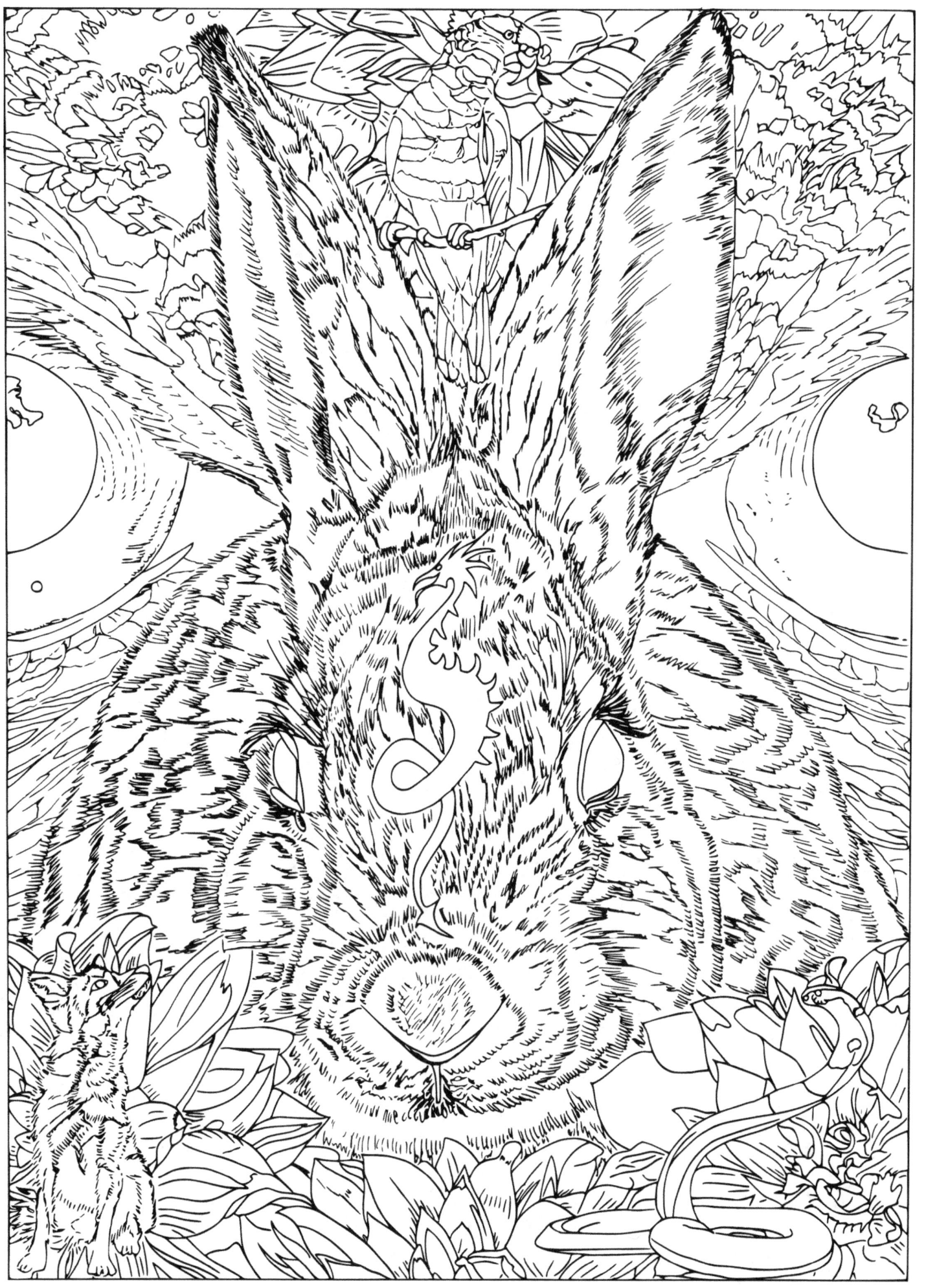

"JungleDreams"

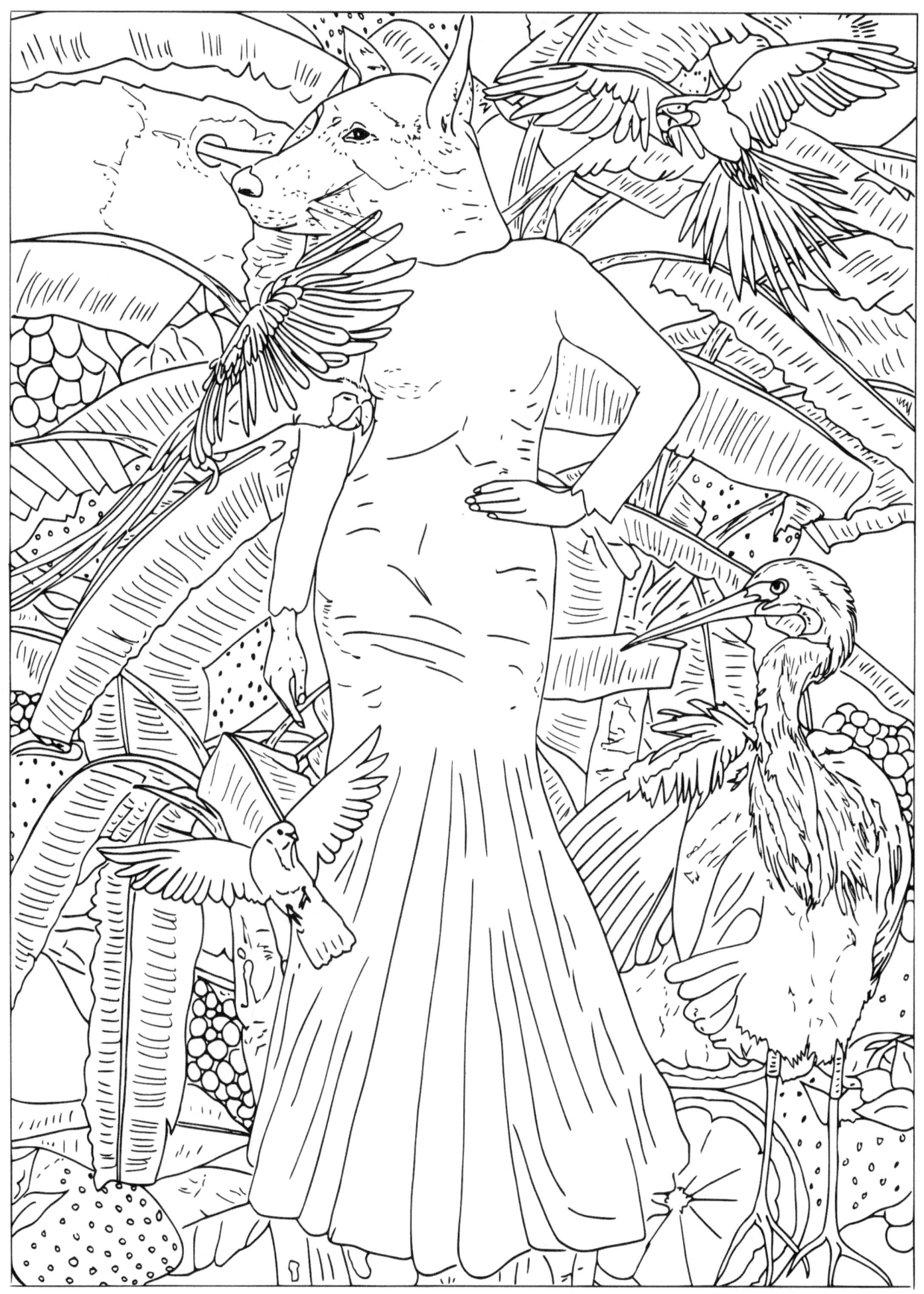

"Kitty Attack"

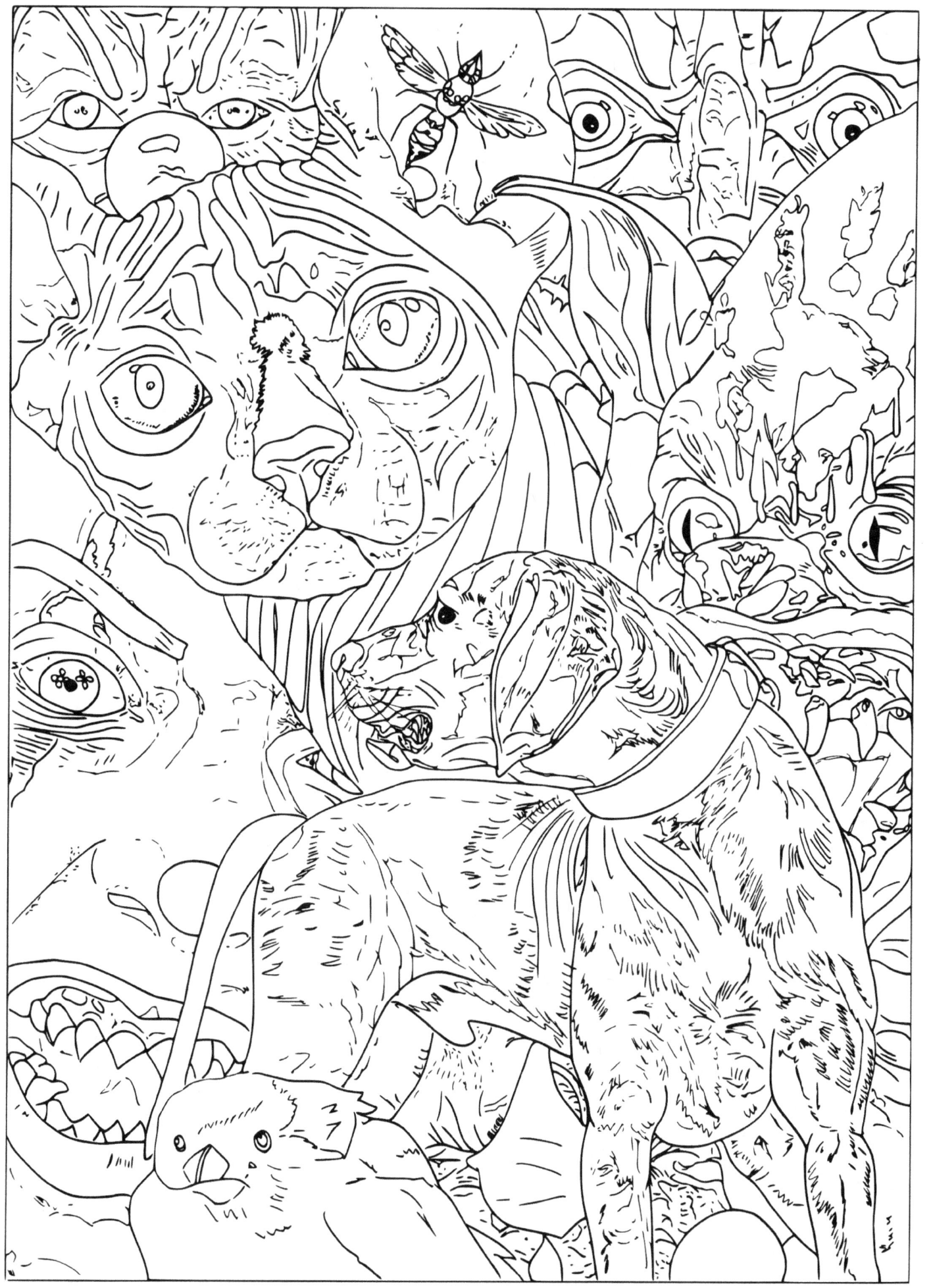

"LionHead"

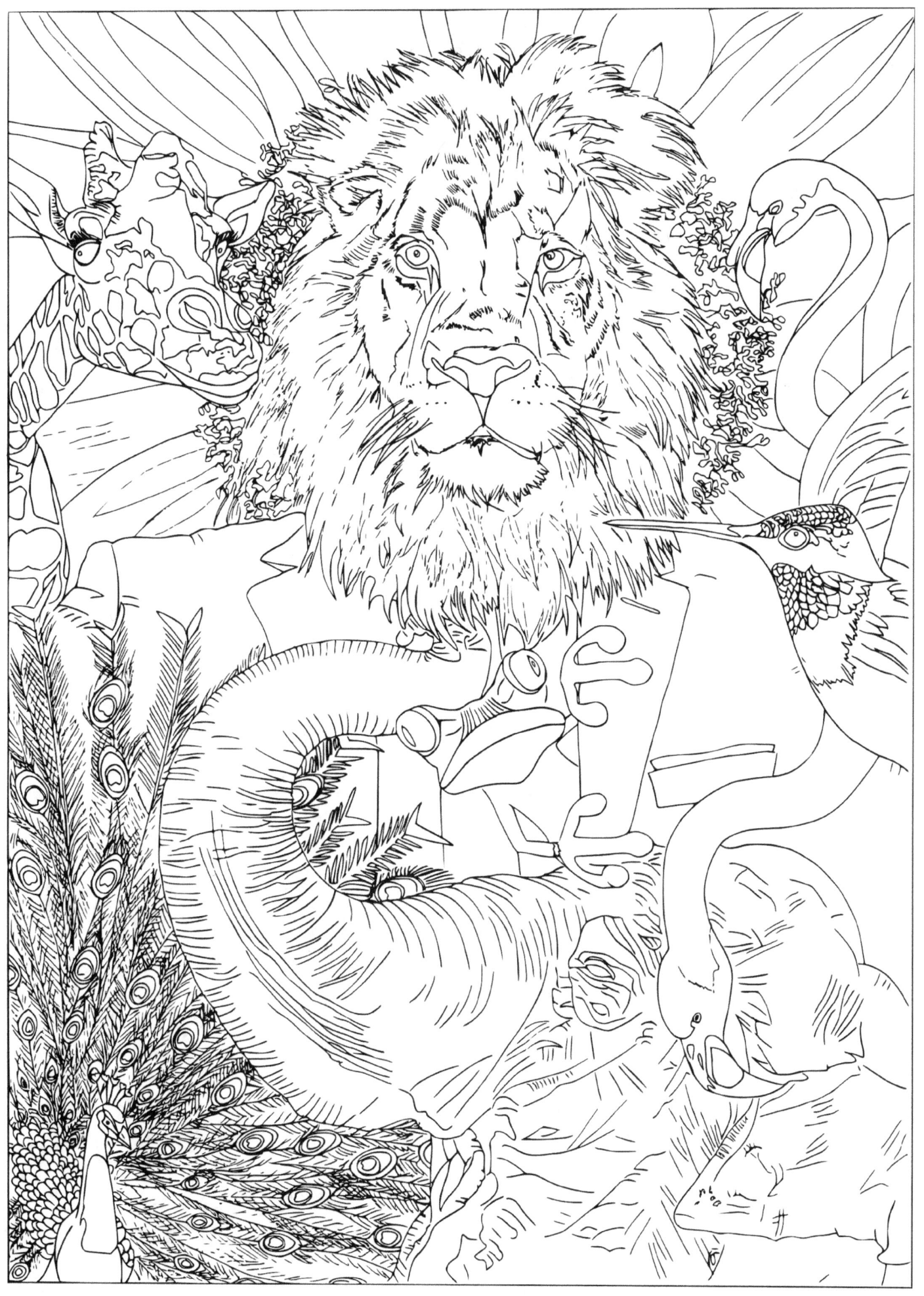

"Lounging"

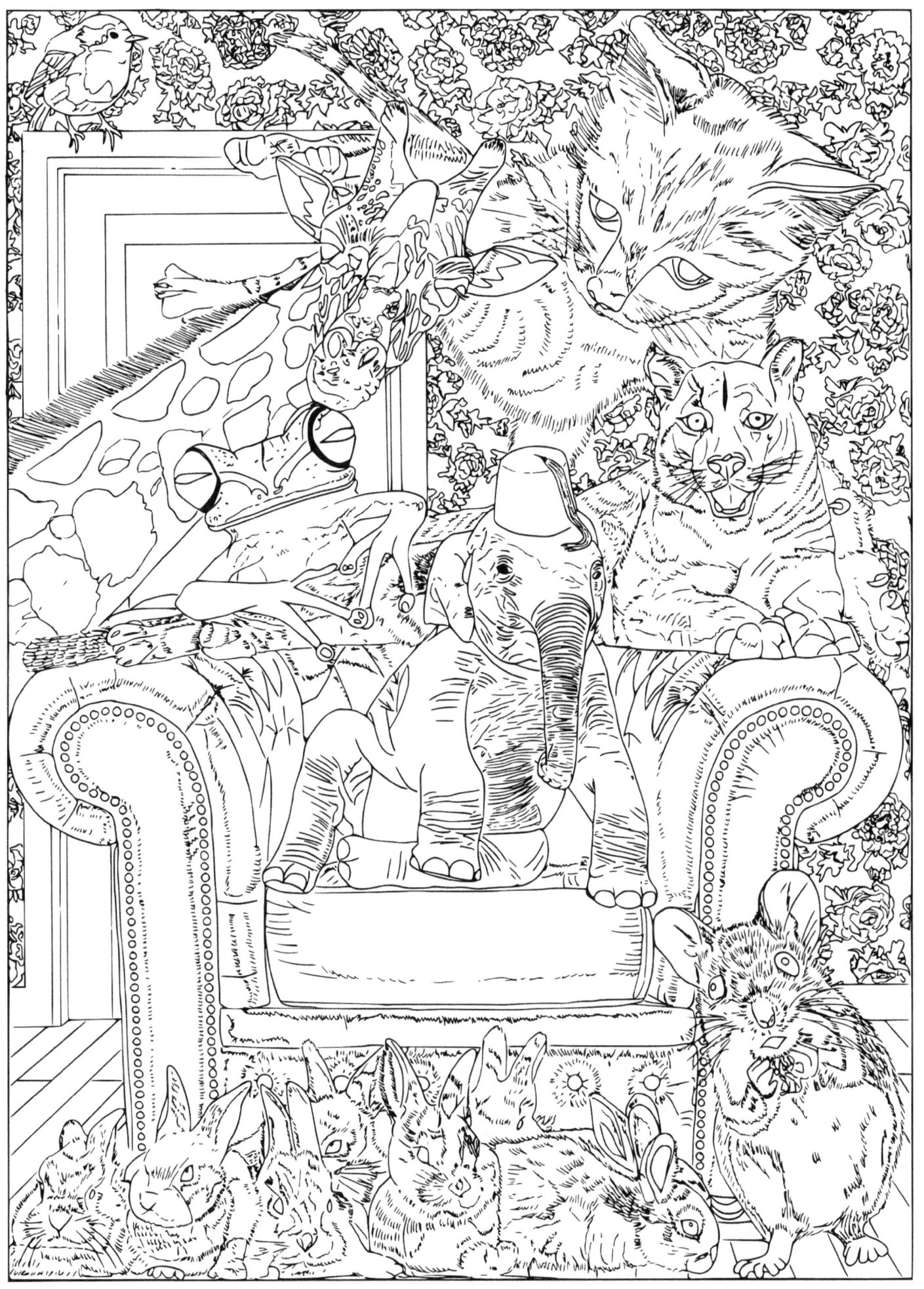

"Monkey Business"

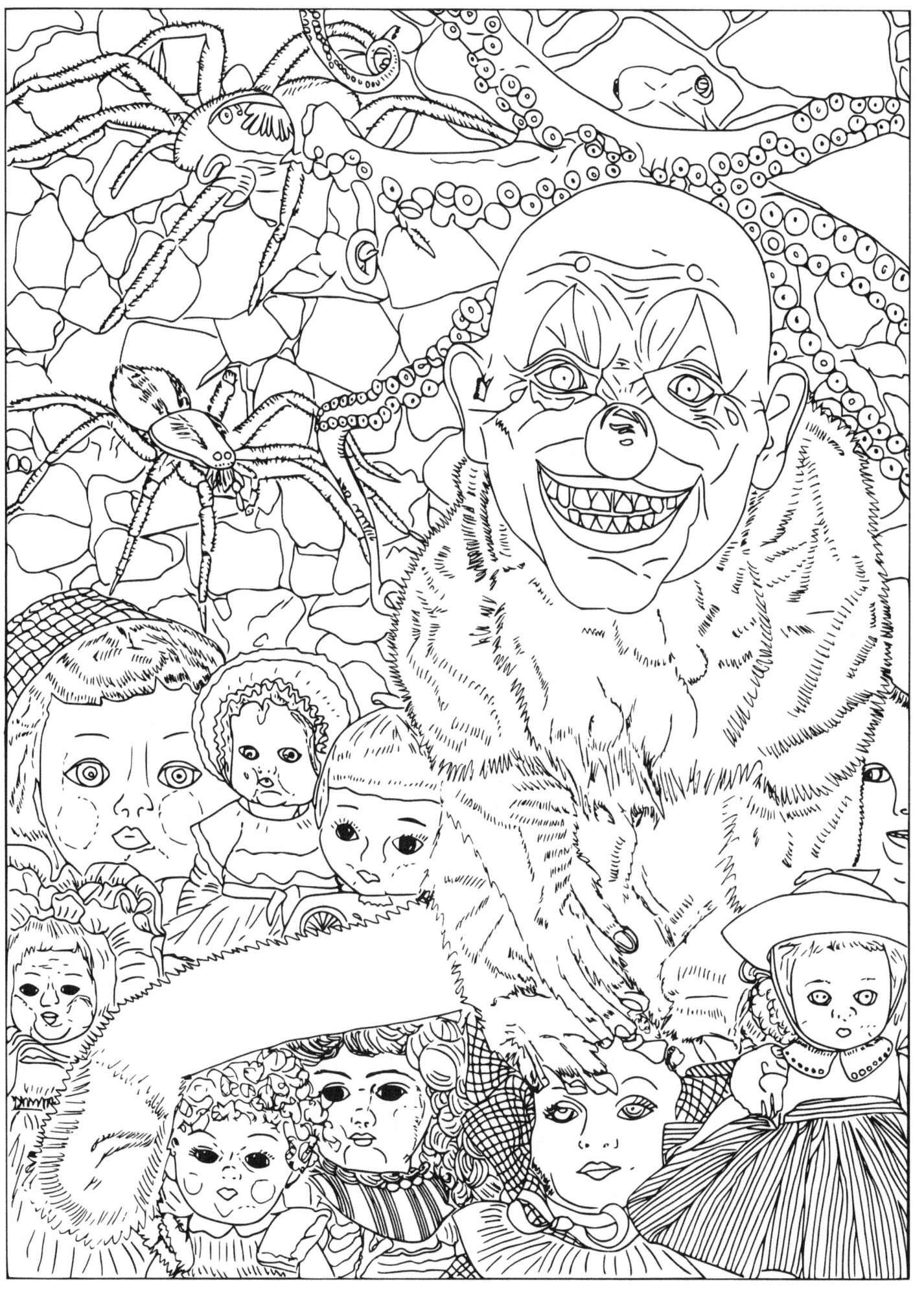

"NothingButFancy"

"NothingButFancy"

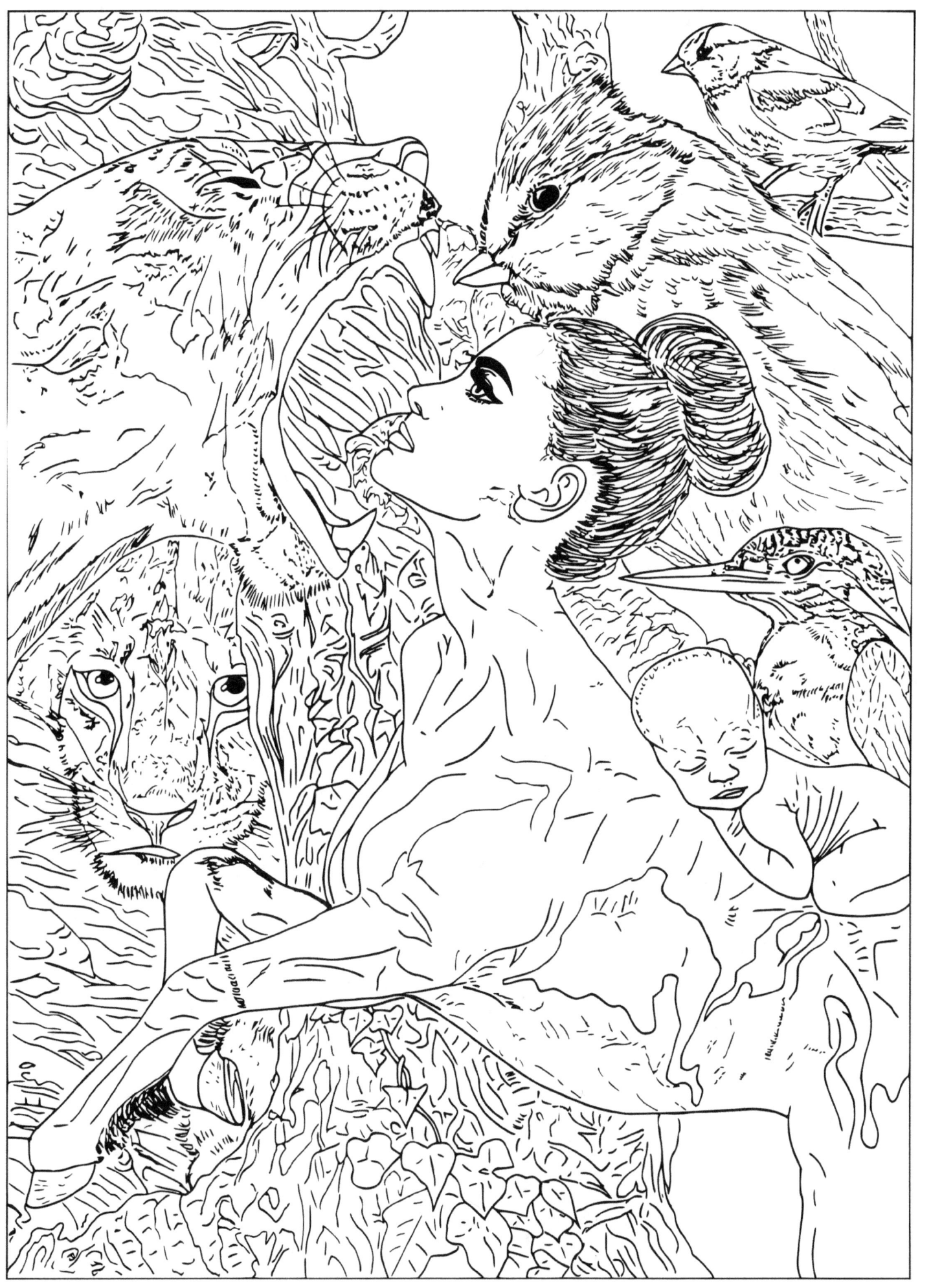

"Pig Rules"

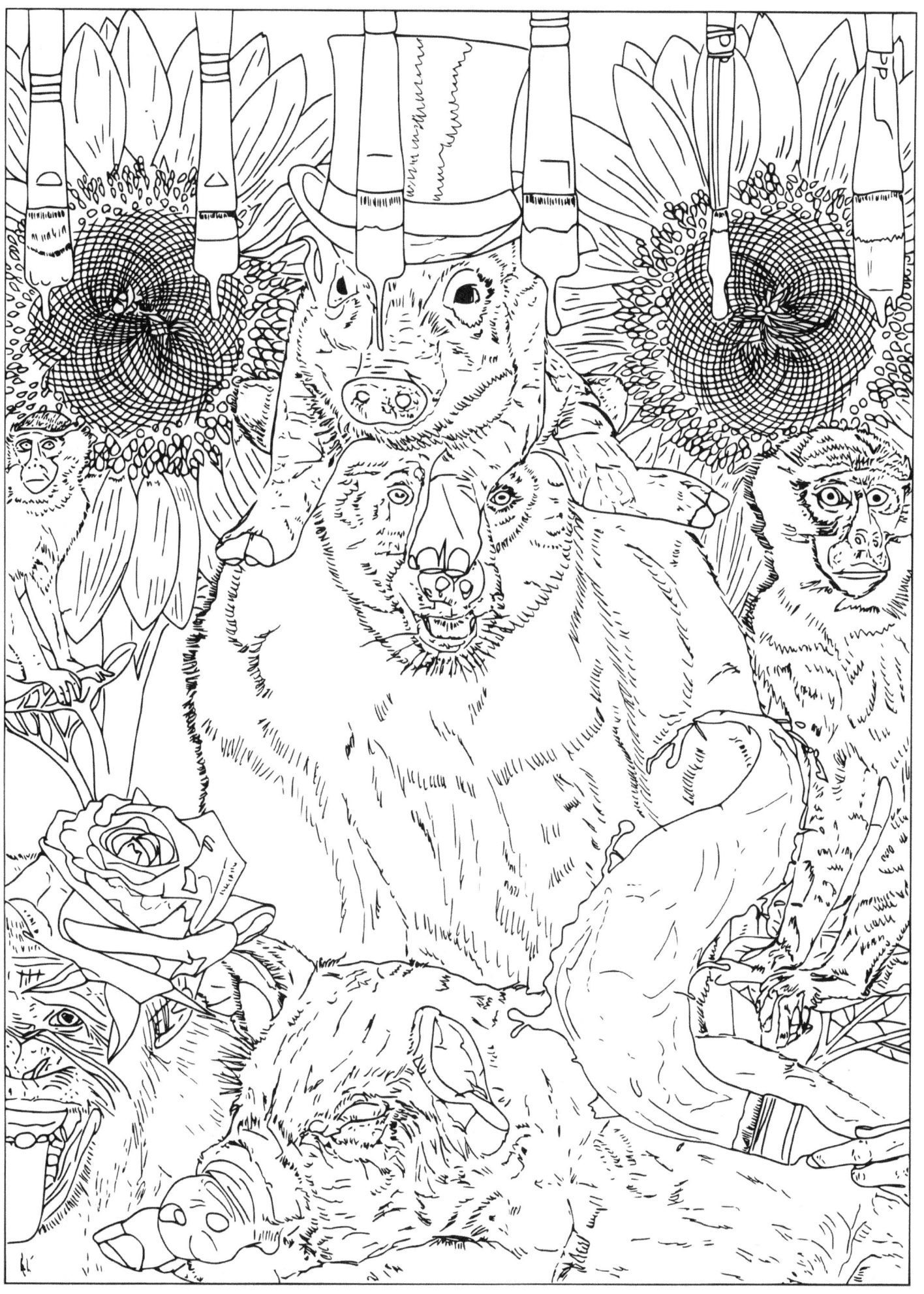

"Rainy Days"

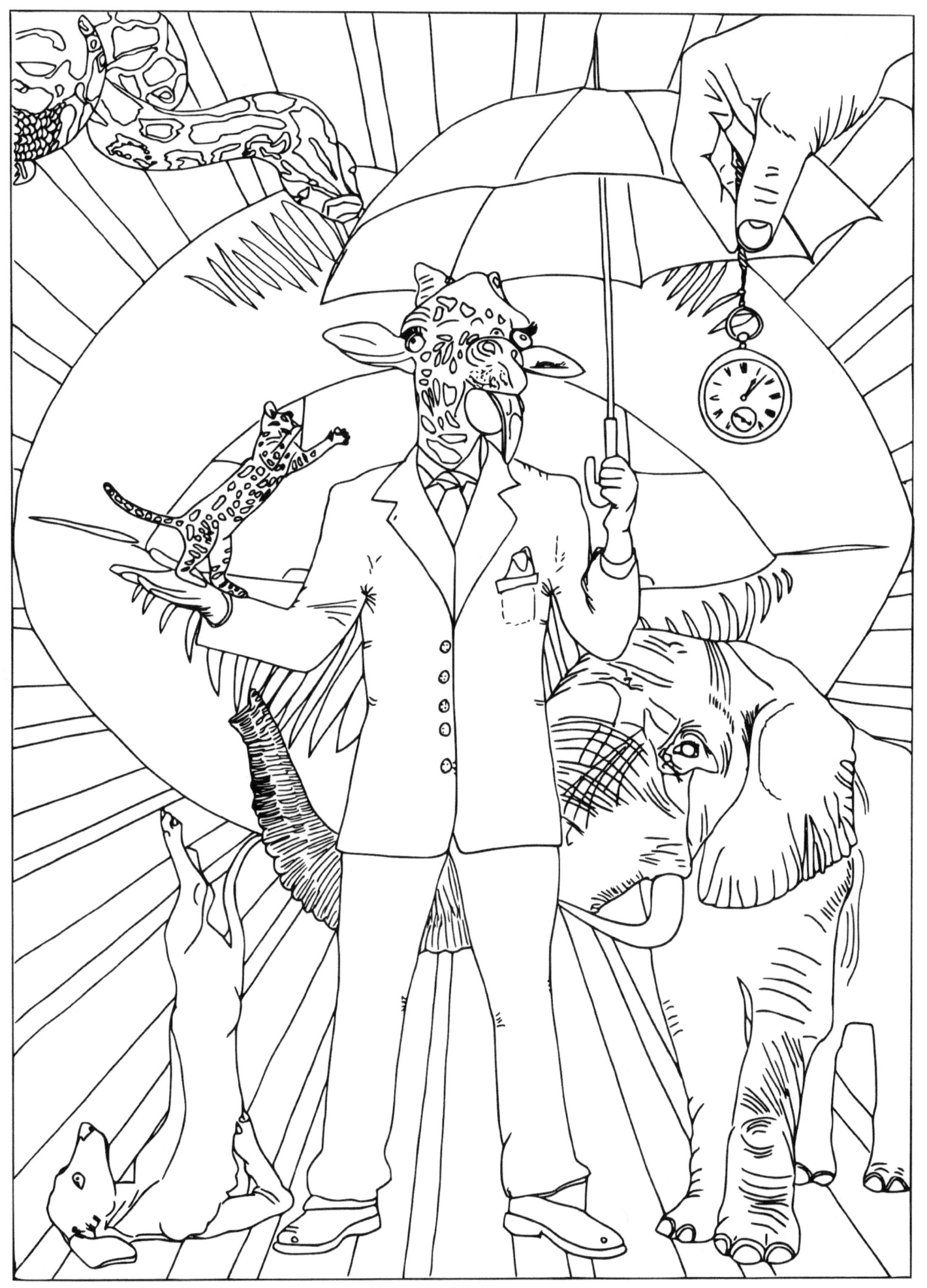

"RoseHead"

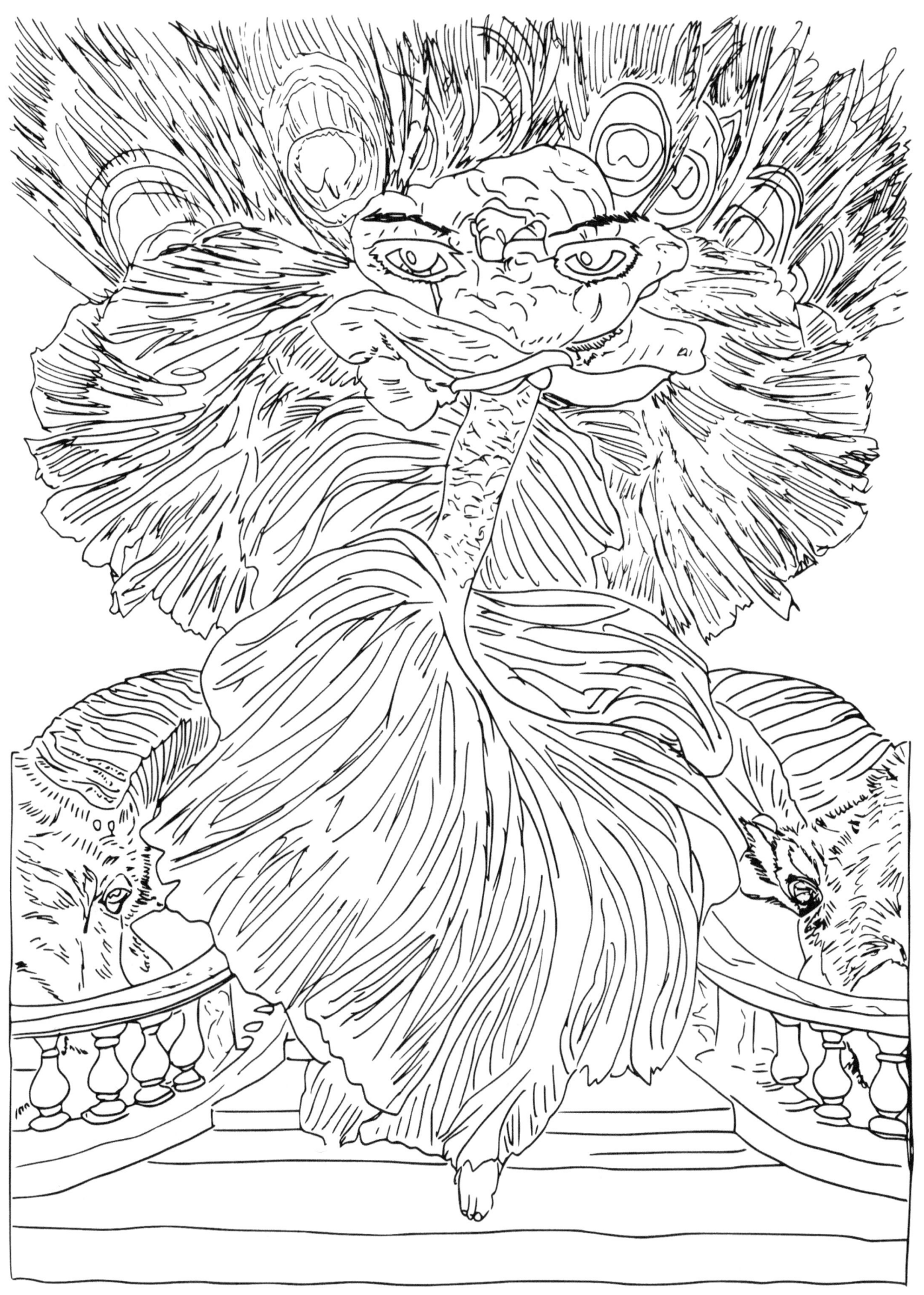

"Scaredy Cat"

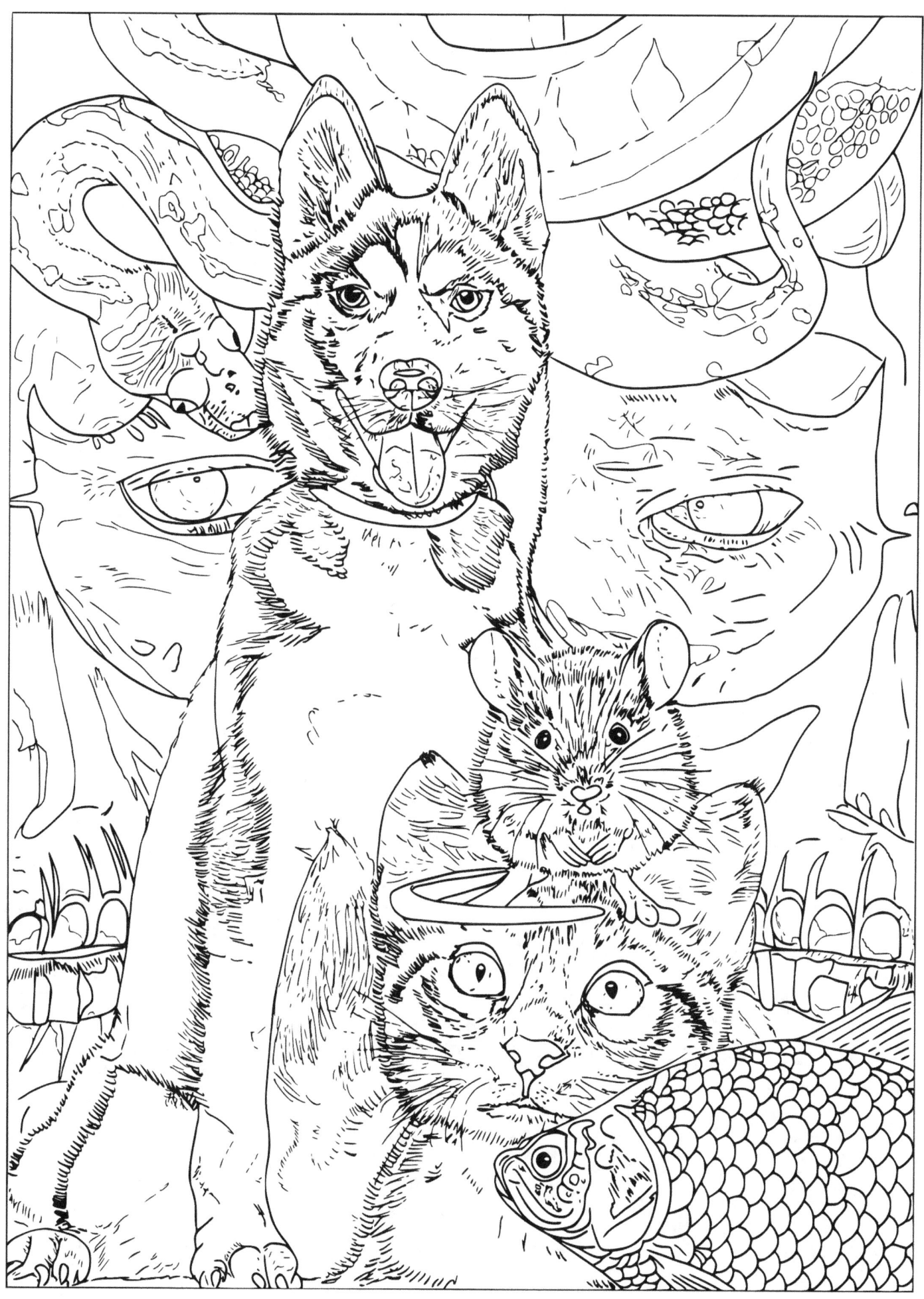

"SharpLeopard"

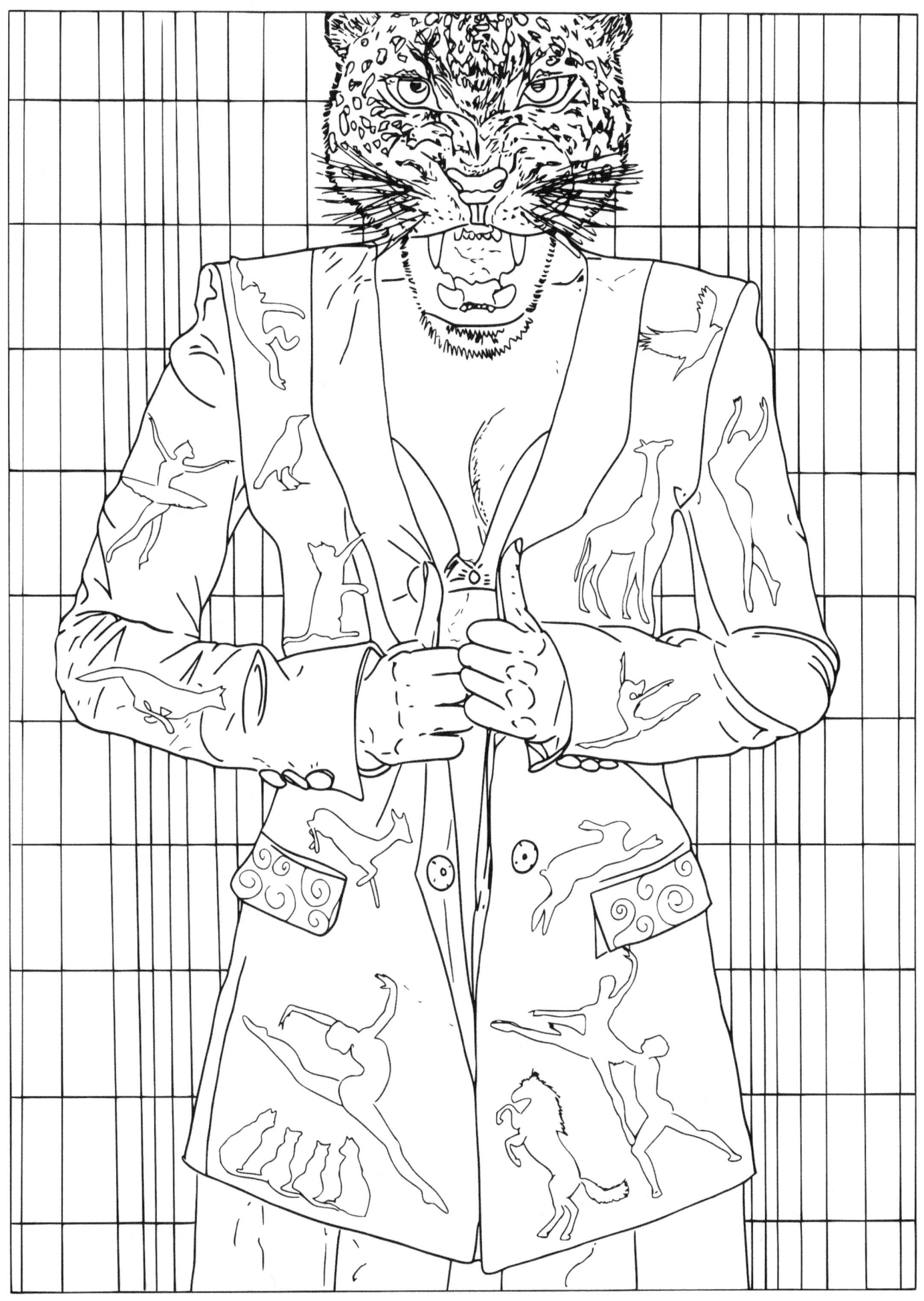

"TigerLily"

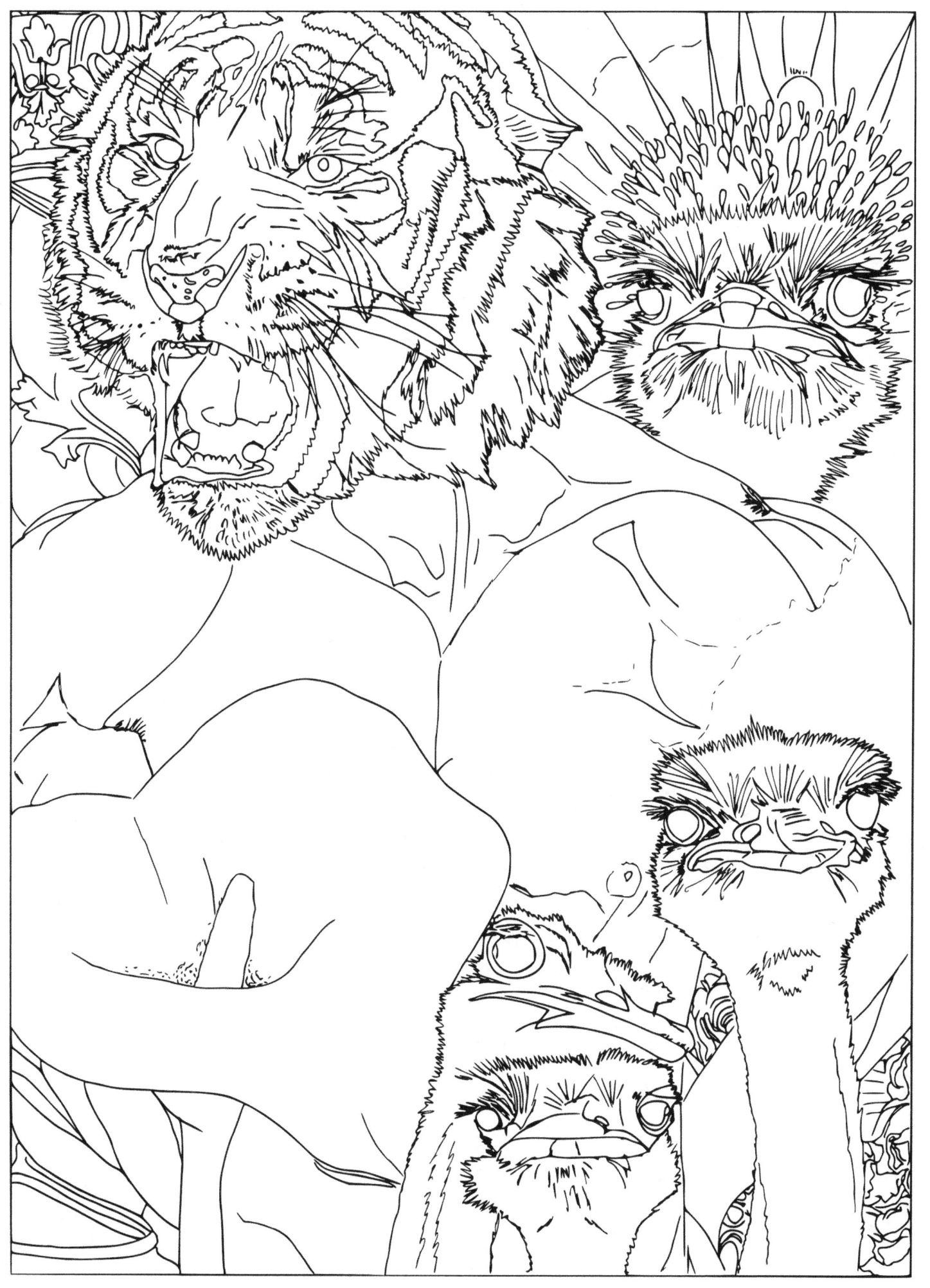

"The Dancers"

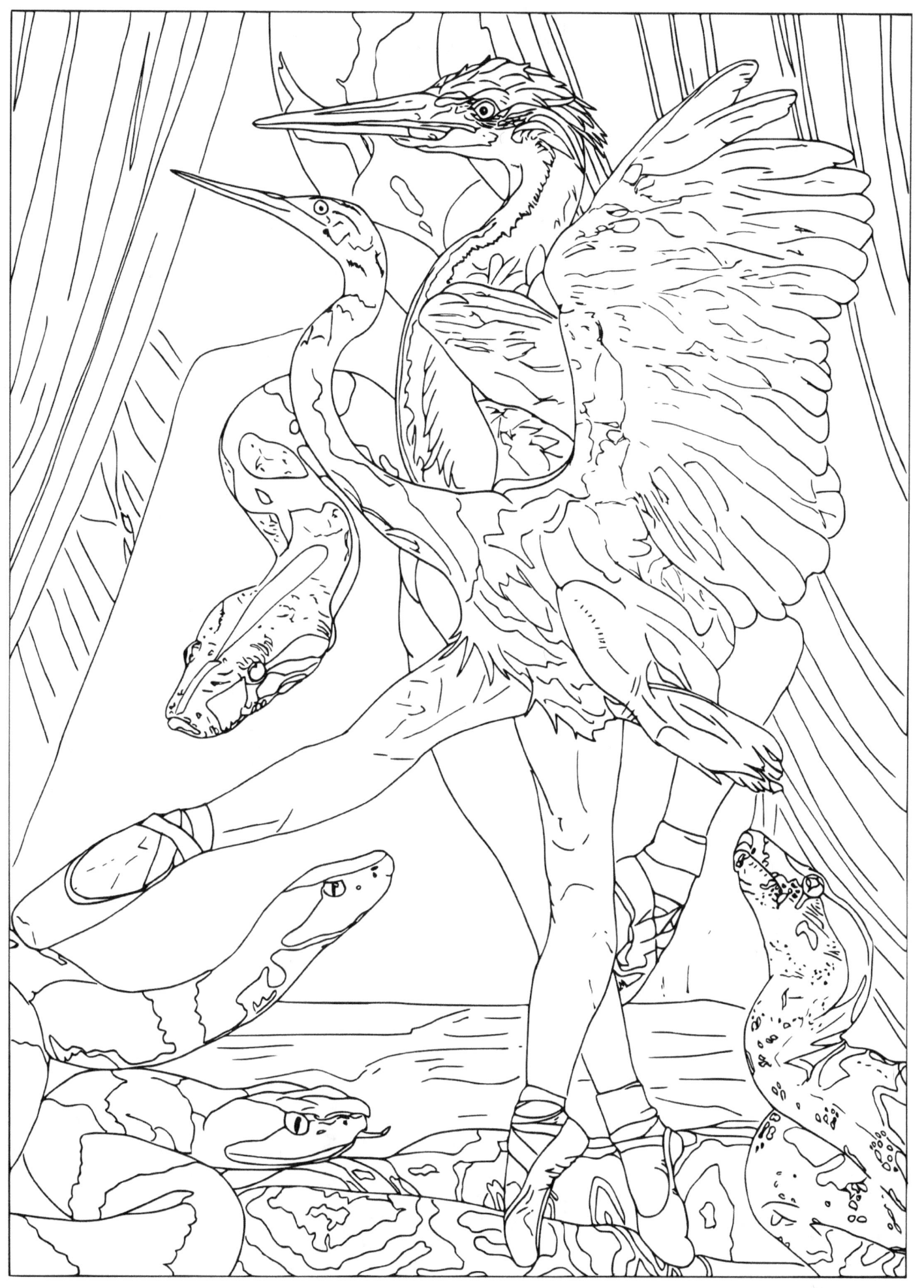

"The Show Stopper"

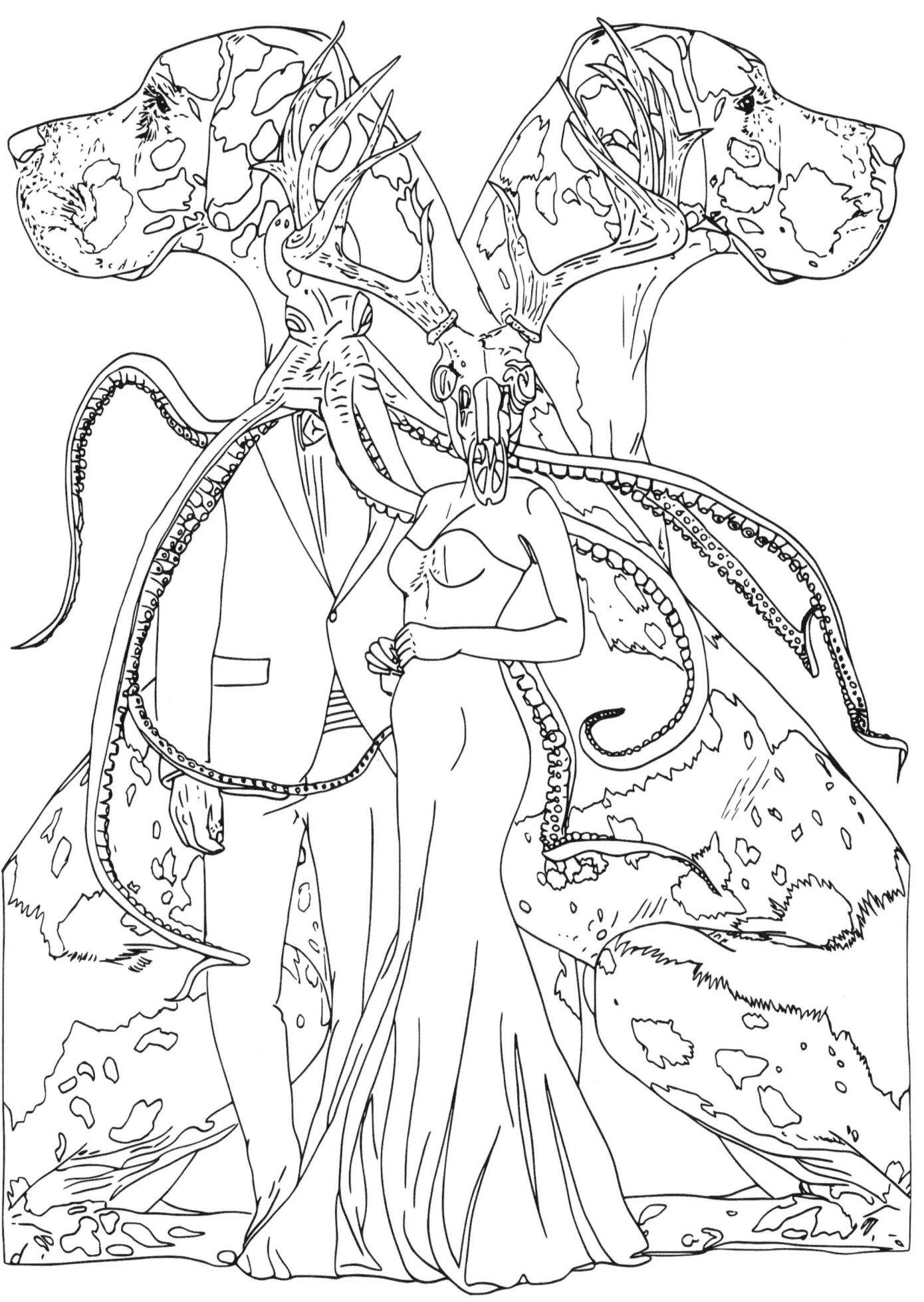

"VintageBird"

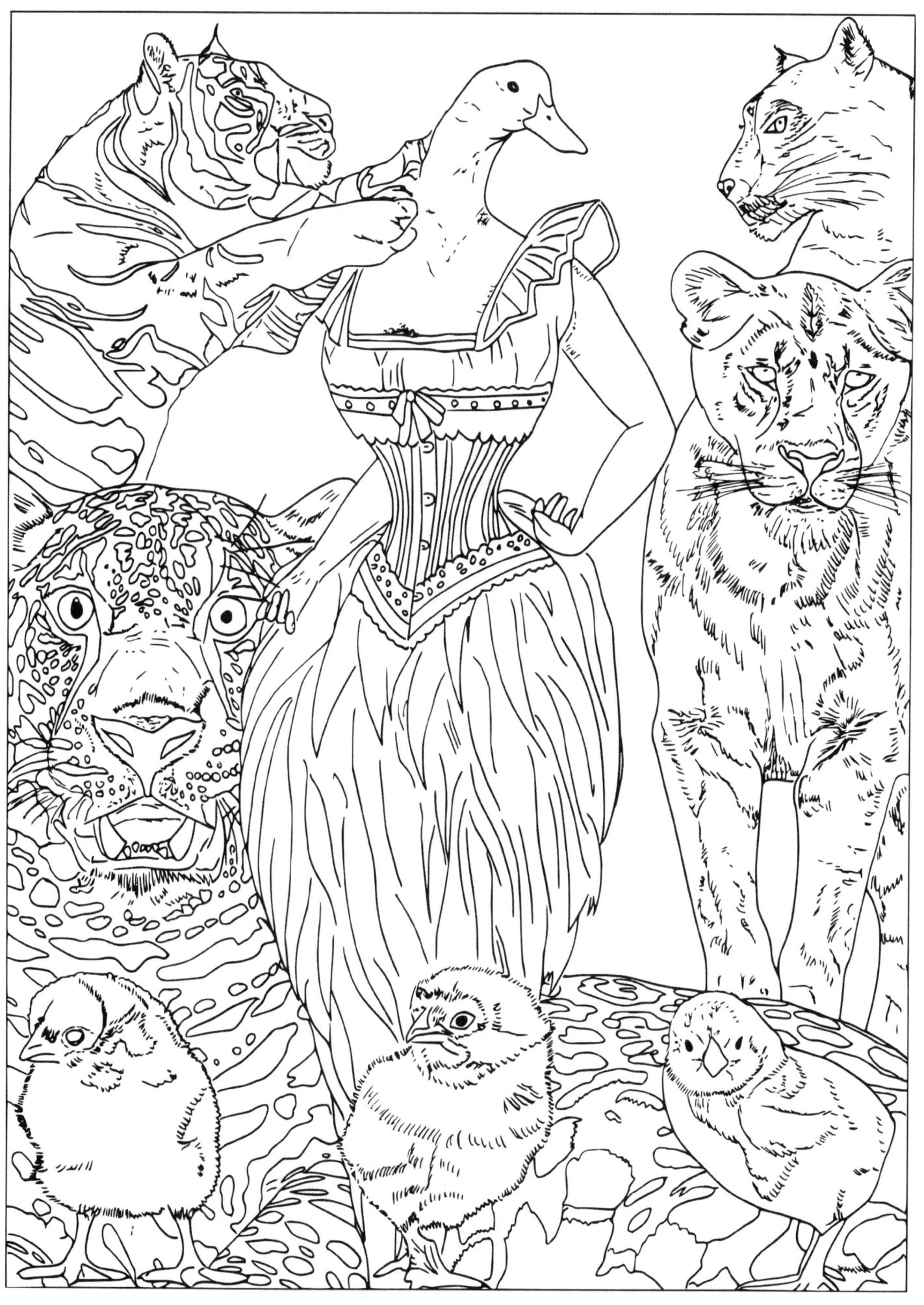

Preview of a few pages from ImagiWorld 2

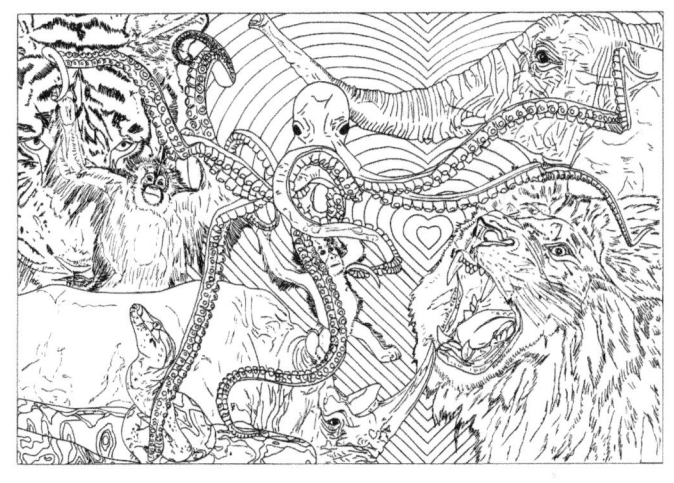
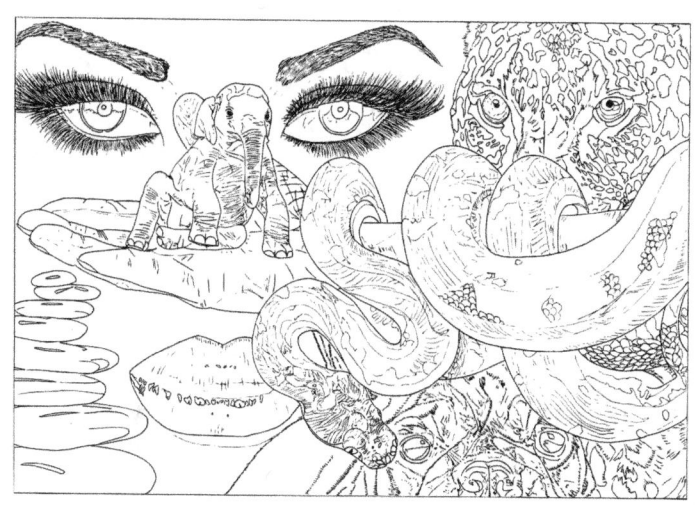
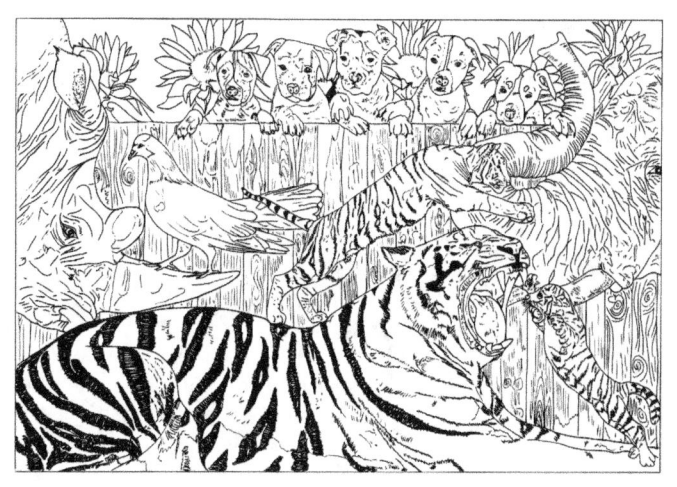
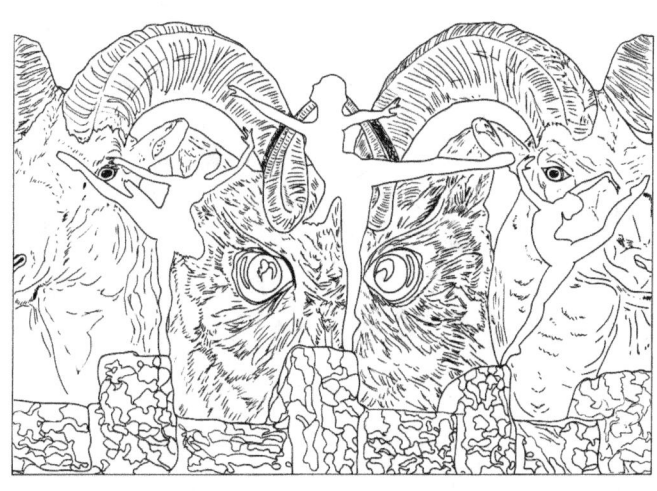
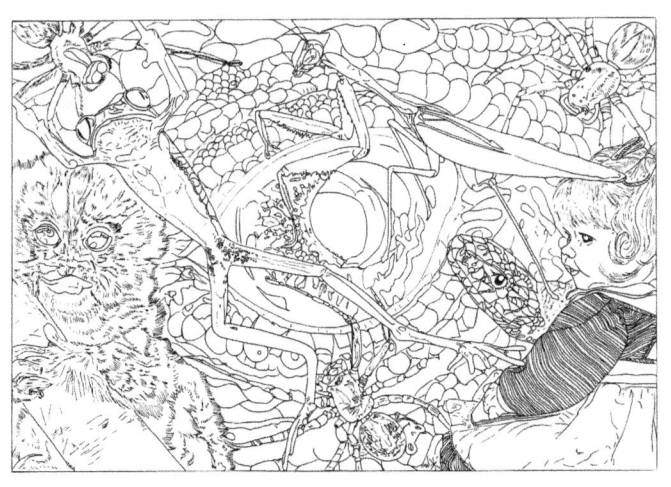
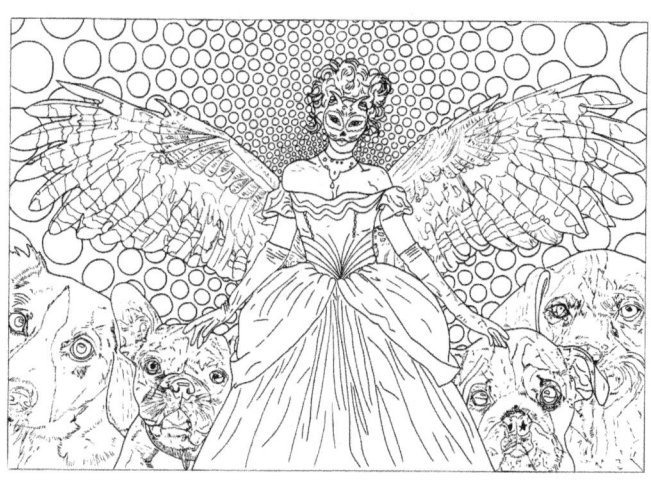

Test your colors here with templates from
"My Color Companion"
by Maria Wedel & Johanna Ans

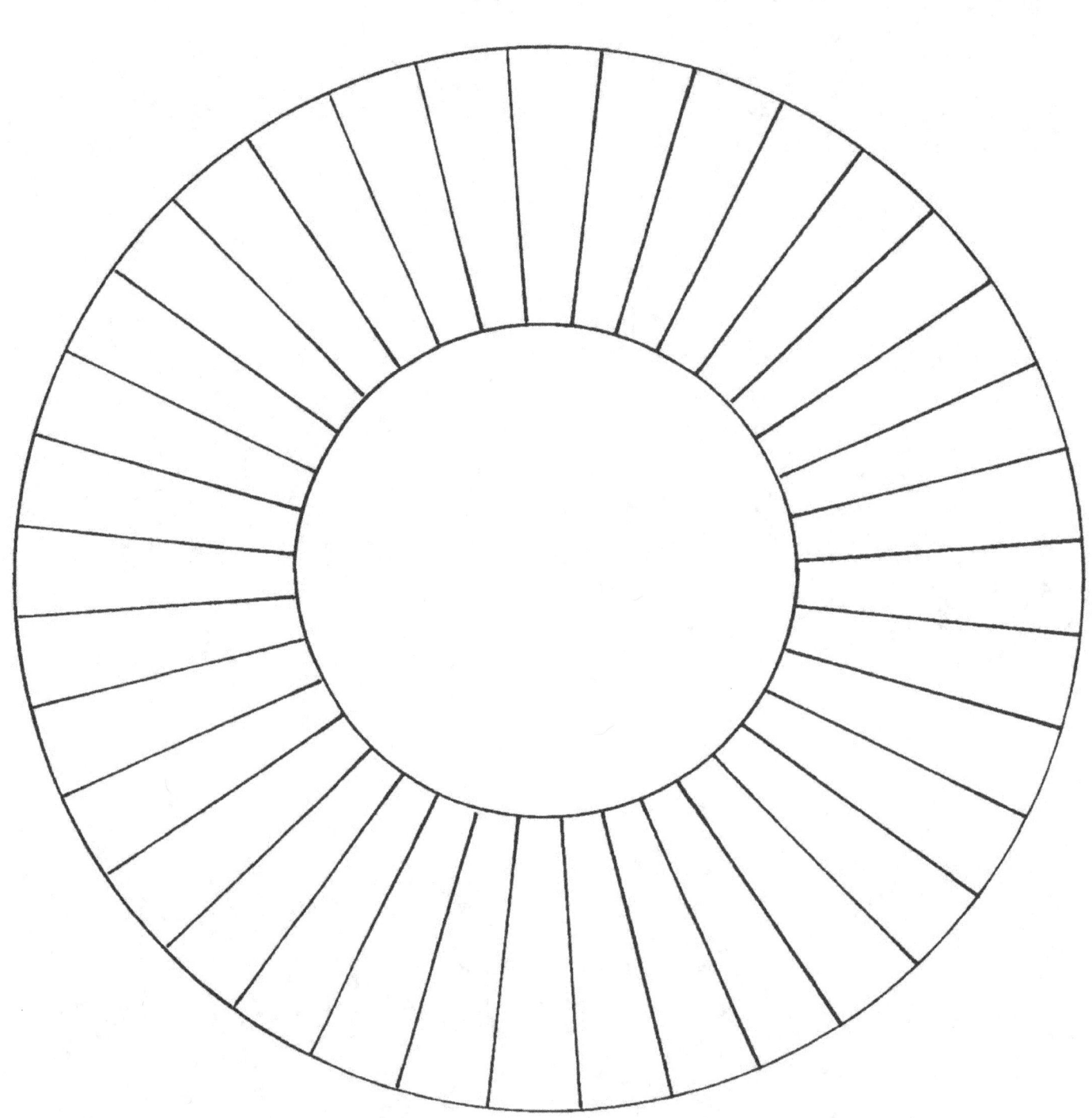

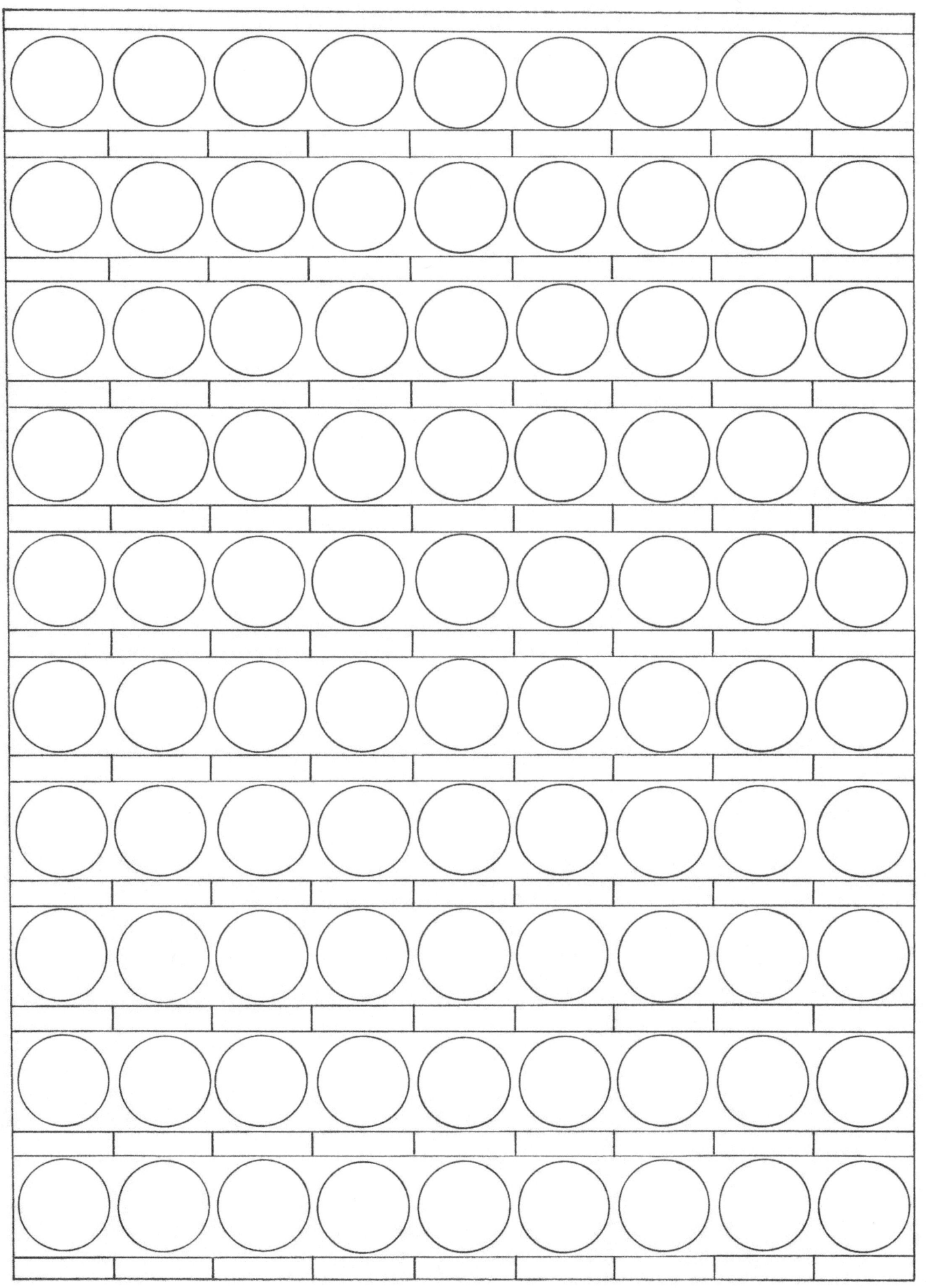

www.ingramcontent.com/pod-product-compliance
Lightning Source LLC
Chambersburg PA
CBHW062200220526
45470CB00009B/2877